Pure Prairie  Plan

Fresh Food, Practical Menus and a Healthy Lifestyle

Dr. Catherine Chan and Dr. Rhonda Bell

Pure Prairie Eating Plan
Fresh Food, Practical Menus and a Healthy Lifestyle

The information in this book is true and complete to the best of the authors' knowledge. The accuracy and completeness of the information provided herein and the opinions stated herein are not guaranteed or warranted to produce any specific results, and the advice and strategies contained herein may not be suitable for every individual. The authors disclaim any liability in connection with the use of this information.

Division of Human Nutrition, University of Alberta
4-126 Li Ka Shing Centre for Health Innovation Research
Edmonton, Alberta
Canada T6G 2R3

ISBN: 978-1-55195-323-6

www.pureprairie.ca

Book design: Tristan Hamilton - www.greeninkgraphics.com
Recipe development: Nancy Hughes - www.nancyshughes.com
Editor: Mifi Purvis
Project management: Heather Loeppky
Food styling: Tony Le
Website development: Patrick Chan - www.chansolutions.ca

Photo Credits:
Alberta Barley Commission, page 20
www.canolaInfo.org, pages 102, 117
Alberta Pulse Growers Commission, pages 13, 55, 70, 158, 166
Canada Beef, pages 78, 143
Curtis Comeau Photography, pages 38, 47, 50, 56, 61, 89, 90, 96, 99, 101, 115, 131, 142, 148, 154, 157
Tim Loeppky, pages 18, 173
Ken Mathewson, Back Cover
Patrick Chan, page 170
Shutterstock, Front Cover, pages 6, 10-12, 14, 17, 19, 21, 23-27, 29-33, 35-37, 39, 41-45, 48, 49, 51, 54, 57-59, 62-65, 67-69, 71, 73-75, 77, 79-81, 83-87, 91-93, 97, 98, 103, 105-107, 109-111, 113, 114, 116, 118, 119, 121-125, 127-130, 132, 133, 136-139, 141, 144, 145, 147, 149, 151-153, 155, 159-161, 163-165, 167, 169-172, 177, 184

Table of Contents

Sponsors

Production of the Pure Prairie Eating Plan was made possible by grants from the following:

Alberta Livestock and Meat Agency (ALMA)
Alberta Crop Industry Development Fund (ACIDF)
Alberta Diabetes Institute
Alberta Canola Producers Commission
Alberta Diabetes Foundation
Alberta Barley Commission
Alberta Milk
Alberta Pulse Growers Commission
Alberta Wheat Commission
Canada Beef
Potato Growers of Alberta

Introduction

The Canadian prairie provinces are characterized by endless vistas of grain and canola fields and it's true that Canada is a leading producer of wheat, other grains and canola oil. But look more closely and an amazing array of other foods presents itself – fruits and berries, delicious fresh vegetables, milk products including cheeses and yogurts, and great sources of protein including meats, poultry, eggs and pulses. Pure Prairie Eating Plan celebrates those foods by combining them into a healthy eating pattern the whole family can enjoy. We hope you find this menu plan useful.

How does the Pure Praire Eating Plan support healthy eating?

Translating the recommendations about what we should eat from *Eating Well with Canada's Food Guide* into practice is sometimes difficult. Taking this into account, we developed Pure Prairie Eating Plan (PPEP). PPEP includes four weeks of complete daily menus, including three meals and three snacks, which incorporate foods produced in the Canadian prairie provinces. In addition to suggested menus, this menu plan also includes recipes, weekly grocery lists, cooking tips and ideas on how to make appropriate substitutions and modifications to recipes.

PPEP can help you enjoy a well-balanced diet while still giving you access to a variety of delicious foods. In PPEP, we provide menus for three meals plus three snacks. The guidelines from *Eating Well with Canada's Food Guide* have been followed and the number of servings of each food group are reported for each day. We also took into consideration the recommendations for nutrition from the Canadian Diabetes Association so this menu plan is suitable for people with diabetes. Including healthy snacks helps to prevent hunger between meals and also decreases the likelihood of overeating at meals or grabbing a less healthy option.

The use of PPEP has been tested in people with type 2 diabetes by the Physical Activity and Nutrition for Diabetes in Alberta (PANDA) research team at the University of Alberta. People reported different ways of using PPEP. Some followed it strictly, every day for several months. Others used the menus as a guide but substituted ready-to-eat or restaurant meals some of the time, or used their own recipes. Still others picked specific meals, like the snacks and the dinners to incorporate into their regular routines. The people who followed PPEP found that it could be personalized to suit their own lifestyles. While research is ongoing, many of the people who used PPEP reported beneficial outcomes, like buying healthier foods and choosing appropriate portions of food, feeling better and improving their health.

Sales of PPEP support further research

The PANDA research team continues to conduct research to help prevent and manage type 2 diabetes through healthy eating and physical activity. Thanks to the generosity of our sponsors, all proceeds from the sales of PPEP will be used to support future diabetes research.

Acknowledgements

Physical Activity and Nutrition for Diabetes in Alberta (PANDA) is an interdisciplinary, multi-sectoral project that aims to improve metabolic control, reduce diabetic complications and improve quality of life for Albertans living with type 2 diabetes. Along the way, the PANDA Nutrition Team developed this menu plan, which was tested by about 100 people with diabetes. Many of those people found it helpful, liked the format and the recipes and thought that it could be beneficial to promote healthy eating for everyone. We would like to thank all of the participants in our research for contributing their time and experiences to the project.

The authors are indebted to the many students who contributed to this work, including Shelly Sohi, Kelsi Ruby, Heather MacDonald, Valerie Friesen, Carolyn Barber, Yu Zhu Liang, Diana Soria Contreras, Gayathiri Durairaj, Denise Maxwell, Saman Iqbal, Lindsay Gervais, Alyssa Harker and Jenny Brown. We also acknowledge the other members of the PANDA team, whose expertise has contributed in so many ways: Sven Anders, Tanya Berry, Sean Cash, Eddie Ryan, Catherine Field, Linda McCargar, Spencer Proctor, Ron Sigal, Jocelyn Ozga and Randy Weselake. We would like to thank students from the Northern Alberta Institute of Technology who undertook marketing research on our behalf: Craig Estey, Dani Young, Kristina Weir, Kevin Van Dolder and Marina Jaminez.

We also thank the talented professionals who made this book come together: Tristan Hamilton (graphic design), Curtis Comeau (photography), Tony Le (chef and food styling), Nancy Hughes (chef and recipe development) and Patrick Chan (website development). We offer very special thanks to Heather Loeppky, for keeping us on track throughout the whole long process and Simone Demers-Collins for her insights into publishing recipe books. In addition to the sponsors listed on the previous page, we acknowledge financial support from Alberta Health Services and the University of Alberta for the conduct of our research.

How to Use this Menu Plan

Pure Prairie Eating Plan (PPEP) uses easy-to-follow menus to help guide your food choices, food preparation, shopping and timing of your meals. You can use PPEP as a guide to achieve a healthy diet and you can adapt and make modifications to the menus according to your preferences and personal goals.

Food choices

In PPEP, we favour fresh ingredients in the menus and recipes and making food "from scratch" whenever possible to reduce the amount of fat, sugar and salt added in many food processing procedures. We suggest using lean cuts of meat and low-fat dairy options. We offer suggestions for ready-to-eat and restaurant meals to make them as healthy as possible (see page 39). No matter how healthy the food choices, though, calories will mount up if portion sizes are too large. All recipes suggest an appropriate adult serving size, and each day, helpful tips are given on how to reduce or increase calories to meet individual needs.

Snack times can be particularly problematic: hungry – but no healthy food at hand. PPEP contains more than 50 delicious recipes and snack suggestions that will satisfy your hunger. Snacks contain at least two food groups and a variety of sweet and savoury options. Many of these snacks are also healthy alternatives for *hors d'oeuvres* or desserts.

Food preparation

Food preparation techniques can alter the taste and nutritional value of food. In PPEP, we've tried to keep preparation simple and use methods that don't add a lot of extra fat or calories. Instead of gravies and sauces, the recipes rely on herbs and spices to liven up the taste. A handy table of common herbs and spices and ways to use them is included on page 15.

Shopping

PPEP includes handy pantry and grocery lists that include the items you would need to make every meal in the book. The pantry list contains items that you can keep on hand for weeks or months, ready whenever you need them. Check through the list for items you already have and then shop for those that you plan to use in the following weeks. The grocery lists are for each week's menus and include mainly perishable items, categorized by food group. We've included lots of different options, particularly in the vegetables and fruits category, to add variety to the menus but feel free to adjust the lists to suit your family's preferences. See suggestions on page 4 for how to make substitutions to the menus.

Grocery lists not only help you to remember all of the foods that you need to buy at the grocery store, they also prevent impulse buying of items that often tend to be high in fat and sugar. The grocery lists will also help you plan a budget for your weekly grocery spending. Copies of the grocery lists are available to download on the website at www.pureprairie.ca.

Timing your meals

Eating three smaller meals plus two or three snacks each day can be beneficial in controlling hunger and cravings, while providing the variety of foods that helps everyone get all the nutrients they need for health. Spacing the meals throughout the day reduces the stress on your body's metabolism that happens when you eat large meals.

Adapting PPEP for You and Your Family: Food substitutions

All the menus included in this menu plan meet the food guide servings outlined in *Eating Well with Canada´s Food Guide*. You can make substitutions in the menus or recipes; just make sure that you are exchanging for foods that are in the same food group. (i.e. fruit for fruit, vegetable for vegetable, meat & alternative for meat & alternative, etc.) so that you still eat the right number of servings of the four food groups.

In the sections below you will find an example of how to make substitutions in the menus using information about the food groups included in *Eating Well with Canada´s Food Guide* with examples of food guide servings (Table 1). A summary table (Table 2) is included with the food guide servings recommended for different ages and genders. For people with diabetes who are familiar with carbohydrate counting, information is included in the back of the book (pages 175-177) on how to use PPEP along with carb counting.

Making substitutions in the menus (example):

If you want to substitute ½ cup (125 mL) of frozen berries in your breakfast for other food:

1. Use Table 1. Food groups and examples of one food guide serving to identify how many food guide servings are in ½ cup (125 mL) of frozen berries. In this example, ½ cup (125 mL) of frozen berries is equivalent to one serving of fruit.

2. Exchange for the same number of food guide servings using the table. In this example, you could exchange ½ cup (125 mL) of frozen berries for one medium fresh fruit, ½ cup (125 mL) of other fruit, etc.

Table 1. Food Groups and Examples of One Food Guide Serving

Use this table to make changes to the menu plan.

Vegetables & Fruit	Grain Products
· 1 medium fresh vegetable or fruit · ½ cup (125 mL) of fresh, frozen or canned vegetable or fruit · 1 cup (250 mL) of salad or raw leafy greens · ½ cup (125 mL) of cooked leafy green vegetables · ¼ cup (60 mL) of dried fruit · ½ cup (125 mL) of juice	· A slice of bread (35 g) · ½ bagel (45 g) · ½ flatbread (35 g) such as tortilla, pita · ½ cup (125 mL) cooked rice or pasta · 30 g of cold cereal (refer to the Nutrition Facts table to see the volume of your preferred cereal that is equivalent to 30 g) · ¾ cup (175 g) hot cereal
Milk & Alternatives	**Meat & Alternatives**
· 1 cup (250 mL) of either milk, fortified soy beverage or reconstituted powdered milk · ½ cup (125 mL) canned (evaporated) milk · ¾ cup (175 g) of yogurt or kefir (another type of cultured milk product) · 1 ½ oz (50 g) of cheese	· ¾ cup (175 mL) beans or tofu · 2 ½ oz (75 g) of cooked fish, chicken, beef, pork or game meat · 125 mL (½ cup) of cooked meat, fish or poultry · 2 eggs · 2 Tbsp (30 mL) of peanut butter or nut butters, ¼ cup (60 mL) nuts

In addition to the four food groups, use the information below to exchange the servings of fats and sugars included in your menu plan.

Oils & Fats	Other
· 1 tsp (5 mL) of oil (canola, soybean, olive) · 1 tsp (5 mL) of margarine or butter · 1 Tbsp (15 mL) low-fat mayonnaise · 1 Tbsp (15 mL) low-fat dressing · 4 olives	1 tsp (5 mL) maple syrup 1 tsp (5 mL) low sugar jam 1 tsp (5 mL) sugar 1 tsp (5 mL) honey

Table 2. Canada's Food Guide Recommendations

	Children			Teens		Adults			
	2-3	4-8	9-13	14 - 18 Years		19 - 50 Years		51 + Years	
	Girls and Boys			Female	Male	Female	Male	Female	Male
Vegetable and Fruit	4	5	6	7	8	7-8	8-10	7	7
Grain Products	3	4	6	6	7	6-7	8	6	7
Milk and Alternatives	2	2	3-4	3-4	3-4	2	2	3	3
Meat and Alternatives	1	1	1-2	2	3	2	3	2	3

General recommendations

· Choose whole grain products
· Choose lower fat dairy products
· Choose leaner meats and foods prepared with little or no fat
· Eat at least two servings of fish per week
· Choose a variety of foods from all four food groups

· Use vegetable oils such as olive, canola and soybean
· Limit butter, hard margarine, lard and shortening
· Limit salt and alcohol
· Satisfy your thirst with water

Portions and adjusting your energy intake

No matter how healthy your food is, it's still important to consider portion sizes to manage your caloric intake. Some samples of servings according to *Eating Well with Canada's Food Guide* are shown on the previous page in Table 1.

Ways to visualize portions:

· *Practice serving out correct portion sizes by using measuring cups or weighing your food.*

· *At dinner, divide your plate into four quadrants. Meat and carbohydrates (pasta, rice, potato, grains) each get one quadrant. Vegetables should fill two quadrants.*

· *A 4 oz (115 g) uncooked portion of meat is about the size of a deck of cards. If you buy meat, cut it into portions appropriate for your family before freezing or cooking.*

· *An average woman's fist or a tennis ball is equivalent to about 1 cup (250 ml), useful for estimating servings of rice, potato, pasta, fruits and vegetables, etc.*

The section "Good to Know" lists basic nutrition information of each day's menu as well as a few simple steps to adjust your daily energy intake. A single energy level does not fit everyone. Use this information to personalize the menu plan and help with your goals such as weight loss.

Measurement tables

Throughout the menu plan, measurements for recipes are given in imperial and metric measures. You can use the measurement tables at the back of the book to make conversions if needed. In order to ensure food safety, a table of internal cooking temperatures is also included. Always use a food thermometer to ensure that meat is thoroughly cooked.

Recipe indices

There are two recipe indices at the end of the book. The index by meal allows you to explore our recipe ideas throughout the day and the index by ingredient helps you use up any leftover ingredients in a variety of recipes. Use these tools in combination with *Eating Well with Canada's Food Guide* or carbohydrate counting to plan your day. Over time, your diet will become healthier and more enjoyable.

Prairie produced foods

Many of the foods used in this menu are produced in Canada's prairie provinces. By eating locally, you will enjoy fresh, tasty and nutritious foods while supporting the environment. Each grocery list has items that are grown locally. Table 3 is a list of foods that are produced in the prairies based on season.

More information about locally grown products is available at www.pureprairie.ca

Table 3. Prairie Produced Foods by Season

	Spring (May-Jun)	Summer (Jul-Aug)	Fall (Sep-Oct)	Winter (Nov-Apr)
Vegetables	asparagus, broccoli, bok choy, green onions, lettuce, pea shoots, peas, radishes	baby potatoes, beans, beets, broccoli, cabbage, carrots, cauliflower, celery, cooking onions, corn, cucumbers, dill weed, fresh culinary herbs, garlic, green onions, lettuce, kale, kohlrabi, peas, peppers, pumpkins, radishes, rutabagas, suey choy (chinese cabbage), spinach, summer squash, tomatoes, winter squash, zucchini	beans, beets, broccoli, brussels sprouts, cabbage, carrots, cauliflower, celery, cooking onions, corn, cucumbers, fresh culinary herbs, green onions, kale, kohlrabi, leeks, lettuce, parsnips, peas, peppers, pumpkins, rutabagas, shallots, spinach, suey choy (chinese cabbage), table potatoes, tomatoes, winter squash, zucchini	beets, brussels sprouts, cabbage, carrots, cooking onions, leeks, parsnips, pumpkins, rutabagas, table potatoes, winter squash
Fruits	rhubarb, strawberries	black currants, choke-cherries, high bush cranberries, pin cherries, raspberries, Saskatoon berries, strawberries, sour cherries	apples, high bush cranberries, strawberries	apples
Meat Products	beef, bison, chicken, duck eggs, elk, farm-raised fish, lamb, pork, wild boar	beef, bison, chicken, eggs, elk, free range chickens, free range eggs and duck eggs, farm-raised fish, lamb, pork, wild boar	beef, bison, chicken, duck eggs, elk, farm-raised fish, free range chickens, eggs, lamb, pork, turkey, wild boar, wild turkey	beef, bison, chicken, duck eggs, eggs, elk, farm-raised fish, lamb, pork, turkey, wild boar, wild turkey
Year Round	cucumbers, eggplant, fresh culinary herbs, lettuce, peppers, tomatoes, artisan cheeses, artisan breads, eggs, honey, grains, quinoa, canola and flax oils, yogurt, milk, goat's milk, lentils, dried beans and dried peas (like chickpeas), butter, dried herbs, craft-brewed beer, spirits, fruit wine, fruit juices, sugar, salt, gourmet sauces and condiments, pickles, jams, jellies, preserves			

Pantry List

This pantry list covers the non-perishable food items and ingredients you will need to follow the menus and prepare the recipes in PPEP. Perishable foods and specialty items are listed on the first page of each week's menu.

Food Group	Food Item	
Baking Items	Baking powder	Flour, all purpose* / whole wheat* / barley*
	Baking soda	Gelatin, unflavoured
	Bran, natural*	Molasses
	Cake mix, spice	Oat bran*
	Chocolate chips	Raisins
	Coconut, flaked	Sugar, brown / granulated
	Cornmeal*	Vanilla extract
	Cornstarch	Wheat germ*
	Egg substitute	
Canned and Frozen Foods	Applesauce, unsweetened	Peaches, canned
	Bean, canned – chickpeas (garbanzo beans)*, / Great Northern*, kidney / white (navy)*	Peppers, roasted, in water
		Pumpkin, canned
	Coconut milk	Salmon, canned
	Corn kernels, canned or frozen*	Salsa, low-sodium
	Juice, apple	Tomatoes, low-sodium – sauce / paste / canned whole, diced and crushed
	Juice, cranberry	
	Lemon juice	Tuna, canned, packed in water
Condiments and Oils	Barbecue sauce*	Oil, olive
	Cherries, Maraschino	Oil, sesame
	Cooking spray, canola oil*	Parmesan cheese
	Honey*	Peanut butter (or pea butter*)
	Hot sauce, Tabasco / Louisiana	Relish, sweet pickle
	Jam, strawberry, low-sugar	Salad dressing, low fat – balsamic vinaigrette / Italian / ranch
	Ketchup	
	Maple syrup	Soy sauce, low-sodium
	Margarine, non-hydrogenated	Teriyaki sauce
	Mayonnaise, low-fat	Vinegar – balsamic / cider / raspberry / red wine / white / white wine
	Mustard*, Dijon / dried / prepared	
	Oil, canola*	Worcestershire sauce
Dry Goods	Almonds, slivered / whole	Pasta, whole wheat* - penne / spaghetti / small shapes (macaroni, bow-tie)
	Banana chips	
	Biscuits, arrowroot	Pecans
	Barley*, Quick Cooking / pearl	Popcorn kernels
	Bulgur	Pretzels
	Cereal – All Bran Buds, Bran Flakes, Cheerios	Pumpkin seeds
	Coffee	Quinoa*
	Crackers, soda / stoned wheat thins*	Rice – brown / instant
	Egg noodles	Rolled oats* - quick / regular
	Flaxseed, ground*	Sunflower seeds*
	Fruit, dried – apricots / cherries / cranberries / figs / mixed	Sunny Boy Hot Cereal*
		Tea bags – regular / chai / herbal
	Granola, low-fat*	Walnuts
	Lentils*, dried or canned – green / red	Wild rice*
	Melba toast	
Herbs and Spices *(See Week 1 for ways of using Herbs and Spices to season food)*	Allspice, ground	Mrs Dash Original Seasoning
	Basil, dried	Nutmeg, ground
	Bay leaves	Onion soup mix
	Cayenne pepper	Oregano, dried
	Chili - powder / flakes	Paprika, smoked / regular
	Cinnamon – ground / sticks	Pepper, ground black
	Cloves, ground	Rosemary, dried
	Curry powder	Salt
	Fennel seeds – ground / whole	Thyme, dried
	Garlic – salt / powder	

*Stars indicate prairie-produced foods.

Grocery List Week 1

Food Group	Food Item	
Vegetables & Fruit	Apples*	Peas, snap or snow*
	Artichoke hearts, canned, in water	Pears
	Asparagus*	Peppers, jalapeno
	Bananas	Peppers, sweet, red / green*
	Basil, fresh*	Potatoes*
	Berries, mixed, frozen, unsweetened	Raspberries, fresh or frozen, unsweetened*
	Blueberries or Saskatoons, fresh / frozen*	Spinach*
	Cabbage*	Strawberries*
	Carrots*	Tomatoes, Roma / grape*
	Cilantro*	Zucchini*
	Cucumber*	
	Dill, fresh*	
	Fruit mix, frozen, unsweetened	
	Garlic*	
	Grapes, red	
	Ginger root	
	Green beans*	
	Green onions*	
	Lemon	
	Lettuce* / Salad greens*	
	Lime	
	Mushrooms*	
	Onions, yellow / red*	
	Oranges	
	Parsley, fresh*	
	Peas, frozen*	
Grain Products	Bagel, whole-wheat*	
	Bread, raisin*	
	Bread, pumpernickel*	
	English muffin, whole-wheat*	
	Pita bread, whole-wheat*	
	Tortilla, whole-wheat*	
Milk & Alternatives	Butter*	Yogurt*, low-fat, vanilla / raspberry
	Cheddar cheese, low-fat*	
	Cottage cheese, low-fat*	
	Cream cheese, low-fat	
	Milk, 1% M.F. or skim*	
	Mozzarella cheese*, low-fat *(see note 1)*	
	Parmesan cheese*	
	Provolone cheese*, low-fat	
	Swiss cheese*, low-fat	
	Vanilla frozen yogurt bars	
Meat & Alternatives	Back bacon	
	Basa (or other whitefish)	
	Chicken breast, boneless, skinless*	
	Deli ham *(see note 2)*	
	Deli turkey* *(see note 2)*	
	Eggs*	
	Ground beef, lean*	
	Hummus (optional; a recipe to prepare hummus is included)	
	Pork tenderloin, lean*	
	Shrimp, fresh or frozen	
	Sirloin beef steak*	
	Stewing beef*	

* *Prairie-produced foods.*
Note 1: Instead of buying a variety of cheeses, pick your favourite. Most of them work well in different recipes.
Note 2: If you prefer not to use processed meats, buy raw or cooked turkey and ham for use in the recipes.

Week 1, Day 1

Meal	Ingredients per Serving	Canada's Food Guide Servings
Breakfast Breakfast Parfait (recipe follows)	1 serving Breakfast Parfait 1 cup (250 mL) coffee / tea 2 Tbsp (30 mL) 1% milk (optional) 1 tsp (5 mL) granulated sugar (optional)	1 Grain Products 1 Vegetables and Fruit 1 Milk and Alternatives
Morning Snack Fresh Raspberry Muffin with Roasted Almonds (recipe follows)	1 Fresh Raspberry Muffin 1 tsp (5 mL) non-hydrogenated margarine 1 Tbsp (15 mL) roasted almonds	1 Grain Products ¼ Meat and Alternatives 1 Oils and Fats
Lunch Tuna Caesar Sandwich (recipe follows)	1 Tuna Caesar Sandwich 1 cup (250 mL) 1% milk ½ cup (125 mL) peaches (in water)	2 ½ Vegetables and Fruit 2 Grain Products 1 Meat and Alternatives 1 Milk and Alternatives 1 Oils and Fats
Afternoon Snack Five Minute Hummus and Crackers (recipe follows)	1 serving Five Minute Hummus 6 whole-wheat Melba toast ¼ cup (60 mL) chopped tomatoes	½ Vegetables and Fruit 1 ½ Grain Products ½ Meat and Alternatives
Dinner Roasted Apple Pork Tenderloin with Roasted Potatoes (recipe follows)	1 serving Roasted Apple Pork Tenderloin ⅔ cup (150 mL) roasted potatoes ½ cup (125 mL) green beans 1 small whole grain dinner roll 1 tsp (5 mL) non-hydrogenated margarine ½ cup (125 mL) 1% milk	2 Vegetables and Fruit 1 Grain Products 1 ½ Meat & Alternatives ½ Milk and Alternatives 1 Oils and Fats
Evening Snack Cinnamon Raisin Toast	1 slice toasted raisin bread 1 tsp (5 mL) *each* margarine, cinnamon ½ cup (125 mL) 1% milk	1 Grain Products ½ Milk and Alternatives 1 Oils and Fats
Total Servings:		6 Vegetables and Fruit 7 ½ Grain Products 3 ¼ Meat and Alternatives 3 Milk and Alternatives 4 Oils and Fats

Good To Know

Nutrition facts of the day	Adjusting today's menu
Calories: 2350 Fat: 59 g Saturated fat: 14 g Carbohydrate: 334 g Fibre: 46 g Protein: 132 g	*To cut about 200 calories* · Have only ½ cup (125 mL) of yogurt at breakfast (saves 50 kcal) · Omit margarine at morning snack and dinner (saves 70 kcal) · Make an open-faced sandwich for lunch (saves 70 kcal) *To add about 200 calories* · Have 2 Tbsp (30 mL) almonds at morning snack (adds 100 kcal) · Drink 1 cup of milk with your dinner (adds 100 kcal)

Breakfast Parfait

Serves 2 - Serving Size: 1 ½ cups (375 ml)

Ingredients:

½ cup	low-fat granola	125 mL
1 ½ cups	low-fat, vanilla yogurt	375 mL
1 cup	fresh or frozen mixed berries, thawed	250 mL

Directions:

1. Spoon ¼ cup (60 mL) granola into 2 tall glasses or parfait containers.

2. Top with ¾ cup (175 mL) yogurt and mixed berries. Enjoy!

About This Recipe: A quick and tasty breakfast when you're looking for something berry delicious. Because of quick freezing options, frozen berries are a good source of nutrients.

Per Serving: 339 kcal, 2 g fat, 1 g saturated fat, 5 g carbohydrate, 5 g fibre, 14 g protein

Healthy Tip: Sprinkle in some ground flaxseed for fibre and a boost of omega-3s (the must-have fats!). For a home-grown Prairie spin, choose strawberries, raspberries, cranberries or even apple slices.

Quick Tip: When buying low-fat yogurt, choose one that contains 1% milk fat (M. F.) or less. The M. F. percentage is often listed on the front of the container. Try experimenting with other flavours of yogurt to see which you like the best!

Fresh Raspberry Muffins
Serves16 - Serving Size: 1 muffin

Ingredients:
Muffin Topping: Optional

2 Tbsp	all-purpose flour	30 mL
3 Tbsp	brown sugar	45 mL
1 Tbsp	oatmeal	15 mL
½ tsp	cinnamon	2 mL
1 Tbsp	lemon zest	15 mL
1 Tbsp	softened butter	15 mL

Muffins:

1 cup	all-purpose flour	250 mL
1 cup	whole-wheat flour	250 mL
¾ cup	granulated sugar	175 mL
2 tsp	baking powder	10 mL
¾ tsp	baking soda	3 mL
¼ tsp	salt	1 mL
1	large egg	1
1 ¼ cups	low-fat raspberry yogurt	310 mL
3 Tbsp	canola oil	45 mL
1 tsp	vanilla	5 mL
1 tsp	lemon zest	5 mL
1 cup	fresh raspberries	250 mL

Directions:
Muffin Topping:
1. In a small bowl, mix the flour, sugar, oatmeal, cinnamon, lemon zest together. Add the butter and blend with a fork until mixture resembles coarse crumbs. Set aside.

Muffins:
1. Preheat oven to 375°F (190°C). Line 16 muffin cups with paper or silicone liners.
2. In a large bowl, mix together all-purpose flour, whole-wheat flour, sugar, baking powder, baking soda and salt.
3. In a smaller bowl, whisk together the egg, yogurt, canola oil, vanilla and lemon zest.
4. Stir the egg mixture into the flour until combined. The batter will appear thick, but resist over-mixing.
5. Gently fold the fresh raspberries into the batter.

6. Spoon the muffin batter into prepared muffin cups, filling the paper cup. Sprinkle the tops with equal amounts of muffin topping.

7. Bake in the centre of the oven for 18-20 minutes or until lightly browned and a toothpick placed in centre of muffin comes out clean.

About This Recipe: These tasty muffins have just the right amount of fresh raspberries with the lemon zest to brighten and enhance the flavour.

Per Serving: 162 kcal, 4 g fat, 1 g saturated fat, 28 g carbohydrate, 2 g fibre, 3 g protein

Cook Once, Eat Twice or More: Share with family and friends or enjoy the muffins another day (see week 2, day 1). Wrap each muffin individually and freeze for a quick grab-and-go.

Tuna Caesar Sandwiches
Serves 4 - Serving Size: 1 sandwich

Ingredients:

2 cans	5 oz (150 mL) each white water-packed tuna, drained and flaked	2 cans
¼ cup	canned artichoke hearts, drained and chopped	60 mL
¼ cup	finely chopped onion	60 mL
¼ cup	reduced-fat mayonnaise	60 mL
3 Tbsp	grated Parmesan cheese	45 mL
2 tsp	lemon juice	10 mL
1 tsp	Dijon mustard	10 mL
16 slices	cucumber	16 slices
8 slices	tomato	8 slices
2 cups	shredded lettuce	500 mL
8 slices	whole-wheat bread, toasted	8 slices

Directions:

1. In a small bowl, combine the first seven ingredients. Spread over four slices of toast.

2. Top with cucumber, tomato, lettuce and remaining toast.

 About This Recipe: Artichokes are a very good source of dietary fibre, Vitamin C, Vitamin K, folate and magnesium as well as a good source of niacin, phosphorus, potassium and copper. This recipe is an easy way to incorporate nutrient-rich artichokes into your diet.

Per Serving: 340 kcal, 10 g fat, 2 g saturated fat, 32 g carbohydate, 5 g fibre, 31 g protein

 Healthy Tip: When buying canned artichoke hearts, choose the ones packed in water. The oil-packed varieties add extra calories from fat to your diet. Alternatively, try lightening the dish with fresh vegetables, such as asparagus or chopped sugar or snap peas!

 Quick Tip: If you are preparing a sandwich (or a wrap) ahead of time, pack ingredients separately and build the sandwich before eating. Removing the seeds from the tomato and cucumber can also help prevent the sandwich from getting soggy.

Five Minute Hummus

Serves 8 - Serving Size: ¼ cup (60 ml)

Ingredients:

1 can	**19 oz (540 mL) chickpeas, drained and rinsed**	1 can
¼ cup	**sundried tomato and herb salad dressing, low-fat or calorie reduced**	60 mL
2	**garlic cloves**	2 cloves
⅓ cup	**water**	75 mL

Directions:

Directions using a food processor:

1. Place garlic cloves through the feed tube of a food processor. Pulse till minced.

2. Add the chickpeas and pulse till smooth.

3. Add the salad dressing and water, pulsing till well blended.

Directions using a blender:

1. Place all the ingredients into the blender container. Blend until smooth, adding more water if necessary to achieve desired consistency.

About This Recipe: Who knew hummus could be so simple? Any veggie dipped in this hummus will become your new favourite!

Per Serving: 35 kcal, 4 g fat, 0.4 g saturated fat, 10 g carbohydrate, 2 g fibre, 3 g protein

---

Quick Tip: When buying prepared hummus, check the label to ensure that the one you choose is lower in fat (<10 g (0.35 oz) fat per ¼ cup (60 mL) serving). Opened hummus stores in the refrigerator for up to 4 days.

Packed with nutrients that help heart health, including fibre, folate, and potassium, pulses (including chickpeas) reduce blood LDL cholesterol (the bad cholesterol) and slightly lower total blood cholesterols by preventing cholesterol absorption in the gut.

In Canada, chickpeas are mainly grown in the southern, arid regions of Alberta and Saskatchewan.

Roasted Apple Pork Tenderloin

Serves 4 - Serving Size: 3 oz (85 g) pork tenderloin

Ingredients:

½ tsp	garlic powder	2 mL
1 tsp	onion powder	5 mL
½ tsp	dried thyme leaves	2 mL
¼ tsp	salt	1 mL
1 lb	pork tenderloin	450 g
1 Tbsp	canola oil	15 mL
1	1 large red apple, about 8 oz (225 g), halved, cored and cut into ½-inch thick wedges	1
1	1 large onion, about 6 oz (170 g), cut into 12 wedges and layers separated	1
1 Tbsp	canola oil	15 mL
¼ tsp	salt	1 mL
½ tsp	fresh rosemary, chopped (optional) black pepper to taste	2 mL

Directions:

1. Preheat oven to 425°F (220°C).

2. Combine the garlic powder, onion powder, thyme and ¼ tsp (1 mL) of the salt in a small bowl. Sprinkle garlic mixture evenly over the pork.

3. Heat 1 Tbsp (15 mL) of the canola oil in a large non-stick skillet over medium-high heat. Brown the pork for 2 minutes, turn and cook for 2 additional minutes or until richly browned. Remove from heat.

4. Place the apples and onions on a foil-lined baking sheet, spoon the remaining 1 Tbsp (15 mL) canola oil over all and toss until well coated. Place the pork in the center of the baking sheet and arrange the apple mixture in a single layer around the pork.

5. Bake for 15 minutes or until pork reaches 145°F (65°C) when inserted with a meat thermometer. Remove from oven.

6. Place the pork on a cutting board and let stand for 3 minutes before slicing.

7. Sprinkle the apple mixture with the remaining ¼ tsp (1 mL) salt. Pull up the sides of the foil over the apple mixture and seal. Let stand for 3 minutes to develop flavours and release natural juices. Stir gently and serve alongside the pork.

About This Recipe: Sautéing the pork before baking seals in the juices and ensures a tender product.

Per Serving: 242 kcal, 11 g fat, 2 g saturated fat, 11 g carbohydrate, 2 g fibre, 25 g protein

Healthy Tip: Serve this with roasted potatoes. Just put them in the oven for about 15-30 minutes before the pork. For a fibre boost, leave the potatoes unpeeled. To add colour and boost your vitamin A intake, make a mix of white, red and purple potatoes. Add flavour to roasted potatoes with a dash of canola oil, rosemary and dill.

Tips for using herbs and spices to lower salt use

Note: To extend the life of fresh herbs, store them in the refrigerator with the stems in a glass of water and the foliage covered with a plastic bag. Alternatively, chop and freeze dry, or make a paste with olive oil, then freeze in ice cube-sized portions.

Name	Herb	Spice	Description	Examples of Uses
Basil	X		Several varieties and flavours, slightly sweet. Easy to grow in the garden (tender annual).	Italian and Thai foods - tomatoes, tomato sauces, pasta and rice noodles, poultry, fish.
Bay Leaf	X		Pungent, slight cinnamon taste. Can be grown as a houseplant.	Bean or meat stews and soups.
Caraway		X	Seeds with a licorice flavour.	Savoury breads, root vegetables (carrots, beets, potatoes, turnips), cabbage, squash.
Chili Powder		X	Mixture of ground chili peppers, cumin, oregano, etc. - may contain salt.	Bean or meat stews and soups; relishes or salsas.
Chives	X		Related to onions - mild flavour. Will run wild in the garden if let go to seed (perennial).	Anywhere you would use onions or green onions. The flowers are edible and a great garnish in green salads.
Cilantro		X	Bright, citrus flavour. The seeds are a spice called coriander. Can be grown in the garden (tender annual, will self-sow).	Mexican and Asian foods - beans, fish and shellfish, poultry, salsas and relishes, salads, vegetables.
Cumin		X	Nutty, earthy flavour.	Mexican and Asian foods, in curries, on poultry, beans and fish.
Curry		X	Mixture of spices, usually hot - variable but usually including cumin, pepper, chili peppers, ginger, cinnamon, turmeric.	Indian and southeast Asian foods - lamb, meat dishes, soups and vegetables.
Dill (fresh)	X		Distinct tangy flavour. A self-sowing weed in the garden.	Fish and seafood, chicken, in sauces, on vegetables such as cucumber, green beans, tomatoes, potatoes and beets.
Dill (seeds)		X	Similar flavour to fresh.	Rice, fish, pickles.
Ginger (dried)		X	Slightly sweet and citrus.	Rice, chicken, marinades like teriyaki. Ginger cookies and gingerbread.
Gingerroot (fresh)	X		Root of the ginger plant - similar flavour to dried ginger but hotter.	Asian and Indian foods. Can be grated and used in place of dried ginger.
Mace		X	Sweet flavour.	Baked goods, fruit dishes.
Marjoram	X		Minty, basil-like flavour.	Similar uses as basil or oregano, also eggs.
Oregano	X		Peppery flavour. A tender perennial in the prairie provinces but can be over-wintered indoors.	Italian, Greek, Mexican foods - especially meat and poultry, meat sauces.
Paprika		X	Related to chili peppers, several varieties ranging from sweet, to smoky, to spicy.	Spanish and Eastern European foods - potatoes, soups, stews, fish, salad dressings. A colourful garnish sprinkled on food.
Rosemary	X		Pine-like flavour. A tender perennial like oregano.	Mediterranean foods - Roasted or grilled vegetables and meats or poultry. An interesting flavour in shortbread cookies.
Sage	X		Strong, musty flavour.	Poultry and stuffing, eggplant, beans (soups or stews).
Tarragon	X		Licorice flavour.	Mild-flavoured meats, poultry and fish; eggs, salad dressing, carrots, tomatoes, mushrooms.
Thyme	X		Several varieties with a range of flavours from lemon to mint. Some varieties are hardy perennials in prairie gardens.	Versatile herb can be used with fish, poultry, vegetables.
Turmeric		X	Bright yellow colour, sharp taste.	Ingredient in curry powders, also in Indian foods, potatoes, can be used to enhance colour.

Week 1, Day 2

Meal	Ingredients per Serving	Canada's Food Guide Servings
Breakfast Quick Cooking Barley Breakfast Delight (recipe follows)	1 serving Quick Cooking Barley Breakfast Delight 1 slice whole-wheat bread 1 cup (250 mL) coffee / tea 2 Tbsp (30 mL) 1% milk (optional) 1 tsp (5 mL) sugar (optional)	½ Vegetables and Fruit 1 ½ Grain Products ¼ Meat and Alternatives
Morning Snack Melon with Yogurt Dip	½ cup (125 mL) cantaloupe ⅓ cup (75 mL) low-fat vanilla yogurt	1 Vegetables and Fruit ½ Milk and Alternatives
Lunch Pork Tenderloin Sandwiches with Tossed Salad	3 oz (85 g) cooked pork tenderloin (leftover) 2 slices whole-wheat bread ½ cup (125 mL) shredded romaine lettuce ¼ cup (60 mL) diced tomato 1 Tbsp (15 mL) fat-free mayonnaise 1 cup (250 mL) spinach ¼ cup (60 mL) red bell pepper ¼ cup (60 mL) grape tomatoes 1 Tbsp (15 mL) low-fat balsamic vinaigrette 1 cup (250 mL) 1% milk	3 Vegetables and Fruit 2 Grain Products 1 Meat and Alternatives 1 Milk and Alternatives 2 Oils and Fats
Afternoon Snack Trail Mix	2 Tbsp (30 mL) sliced almonds 1 Tbsp (15 mL) sunflower seeds 2 Tbsp (30 mL) dried apricots 1 Tbsp (15 mL) dried banana chips	¾ Vegetables and Fruit ½ Meat and Alternatives
Dinner Roasted Vegetable Penne Bake and Grilled Chicken (recipes follow)	1 serving Roasted Vegetable Penne Bake 3 oz (85 g) chicken breast ½ cup (125 mL) 1% milk	4 Vegetables and Fruit 1 ½ Grain Products 1 Meat and Alternatives ¾ Milk and Alternatives 2 ½ Oils and Fats
Evening Snack Applesauce Raisin Cookies and Milk (recipe follows)	2 Applesauce Raisin Cookies ½ cup (125 mL) 1% milk	2 Grain Products ½ Milk and Alternatives
Total Servings:		9 ¼ Vegetables and Fruit 7 Grain Products 2 ¾ Meat and Alternatives 2 ¾ Milk and Alternatives 4 ½ Oils and Fats

Good To Know

Nutrition facts of the day	Adjusting today's menu
Calories: 1728 g Fat: 61 g Saturated fat: 13 g Carbohydrate: 220 g Fibre: 30 g Protein: 84 g	*To cut about 200 calories* · Have an open-faced sandwich at lunch, decreasing bread by 1 slice (saves 80 kcal) · Omit salad at lunch (saves 70 kcal) · Have only 1 cookie at evening snack (saves 50 kcal) *To add about 200 calories* · Increase yogurt to ¾ cup (175 mL) for morning snack (adds 90 kcal) · Add an extra Tbsp salad dressing to tossed salad (adds 50 kcal) · Have 4 oz (115 g) chicken for dinner (adds 50 kcal)

Quick Cooking Barley Breakfast Delight

Serves 5 - Serving Size: ¾ cup (175 ml)

Ingredients:

1 cup	quick-cooking barley	250 mL
¾ cup	water	175 mL
½ cup	apple juice	125 mL
½ tsp	cinnamon	2 mL
¼ tsp	nutmeg	1 mL
¼ cup	almonds slivered	60 mL
3 Tbsp	raisins	45 mL
¼ cup	dried figs, cranberries or apricots	60 mL

Directions:

1. Combine the ingredients and bring to a boil in a heavy medium saucepan. Reduce heat and simmer for up to 15 minutes, stirring frequently.

2. Remove from heat and serve with milk and brown sugar. This recipe can be made ahead of time and kept in the refrigerator and reheated in the microwave oven.

About This Recipe: Cholesterol lowering barley paired with warm spices and dried fruit? That is how you want to start your morning.

Per Serving: 217 kcal, 4 g fat, 0.5 g saturated fat, 39 g carbohydrate, 8 g fibre, 7 g protein

Healthy Tip: Barley is a grain product with low glycemic index (GI) that raises your blood sugar levels slowly and steadily. Other low-GI grains include bulgur, whole-wheat pasta and parboiled rice. Choose these more often than high-GI grains such as short-grain rice.

Quick Tip: If quick-cooking barley isn't available, use regular barley and extend the cooking time according to package directions. Check www.pureprairie.ca for where to buy quick-cooking barley.

Roasted Vegetable Penne Bake

Serves 6 - Serving Size: 1 square

Ingredients:

2	large zucchinis, cut into 1-inch (2.5 cm) pieces	2
1	medium sweet red pepper, cut into 1-inch (2.5 cm) pieces	1
1	small onion, cut into 1-inch (2.5 cm) pieces	1
½ lb	medium fresh mushrooms, halved	225 g
2 Tbsp	olive oil	30 mL
1 ½ tsp	Italian seasoning	7 mL
2 cups	uncooked penne pasta	500 mL
1 can	14 oz (398 mL) crushed tomatoes, undrained	1 can
2 oz	shredded provolone cheese	60 g
¾ cup	frozen peas, thawed	175 mL
¼ cup	shredded part-skim mozzarella cheese	60 mL
3 Tbsp	grated Parmesan cheese	45 mL
½ tsp	salt	2 mL
½ tsp	pepper	2 mL
1 Tbsp	butter or margarine	15 mL
1 Tbsp	grated Parmesan cheese	15 mL

Directions:

1. In a large bowl, combine the zucchini, red pepper, mushrooms, onion, oil and Italian seasoning; toss to coat. Arrange in a single layer on an ungreased 15-inch (38 x 25 cm) baking pan. Bake, uncovered, at 425°F (220 °C) for 20-25 minutes or until tender.

2. Meanwhile, cook pasta according to package directions; drain. In a large bowl, combine the pasta, roasted vegetables, tomatoes, provolone cheese, peas, mozzarella cheese, ¼ cup (60 mL) Parmesan cheese, and salt and pepper.

3. Transfer to a greased 11 x 7 inch (28 x 43 cm) baking dish. Sprinkle with remaining Parmesan cheese; dot with butter. Cover and bake at 350°F (180°C) for 10 minutes. Uncover; bake for another 10-15 minutes or until bubbly.

4. Cut into six squares and garnish with fresh herbs, if available.

About This Recipe: Get your veggies in a delicious way with this vegetable bake! There are also three types of cheeses in this recipe. Need I say more?

Per Serving: 317 kcal, 12 g fat, 5 g saturated fat, 33 g carbohydrate, 6 g fibre, 13 g protein

Basic Grilled Chicken

Serves 3 - Serving Size: 3 oz (85 g)

Ingredients:

9 oz	boneless, skinless chicken breast	250 g
2 Tbsp	canola oil	30 mL
2 Tbsp	lemon juice	30 mL
	onion salt and pepper to taste	
pinch	dry parsley	pinch

Directions:

1. In a medium bowl, combine canola oil and lemon juice. Dip chicken breast into mixture. Coat both sides.

2. Transfer chicken breast to a hot non-stick frying pan. Sprinkle with onion salt and pepper. Fry over medium to high heat until an internal temperature of 170°F (77°C) is reached (about 3 ½ minutes on each side depending on the thickness of the chicken breast).

3. Garnish with parsley prior to serving.

About This Recipe: Need a side of protein on your dish? Look no further than this clean, classic chicken dish.

Per Serving: 199 kcal, 13 g fat, 1 g saturated fat, 1 g carbohydrate, 0 fibre, 20 g protein.

Chef's Tip: A great way to dress up chicken breasts, pasta, potato salad and more is by using herb pastes. Be aware that herb pastes add extra oil and add sparingly.

The prairie provinces produce about one-sixth of the chickens grown in Canada and about one-fifth of the turkeys. In the last 20 years, chicken meat has become a favourite of Canadians, both in home-cooking and restaurant meals.

Applesauce Raisin Cookies

Serves 18 - Serving Size: 1 cookie

Ingredients:

¼ cup	applesauce	60 mL
¼ cup	canola oil	60 mL
½ cup	brown sugar	125 mL
1	egg	1
½ tsp	baking soda	2 mL
½ tsp	salt	2 mL
½ tsp	cinnamon	2 mL
¼ tsp	ginger	1 mL
¼ tsp	nutmeg	1 mL
½ tsp	vanilla	2 mL
1 cup	rolled oats	250 mL
⅞ cup	whole barley flour	225 mL
½ cup	raisins	125 mL

Directions:

1. In a large bowl, cream together applesauce, canola oil and brown sugar.

2. Beat in egg.

3. Add remaining ingredients and mix until well combined.

4. Drop by spoonfuls on a greased cookie sheet.

5. Bake for 10-12 minutes at 350°F (180°C).

About This Recipe: This tasty cookie is full of flavour, moisture and nutrients from the applesauce, rolled oats and barley flour!

Per Serving: 104 kcal, 4 g fat, 0.3 g saturated fat, 16 g carbohydrate, 1 g fibre, 2 g protein

Cook Once, Eat Twice or More: Double wrap the cookies and freeze. You can keep them up to 3-4 weeks in the freezer.

To make a batch of your own unsweetened applesauce:
Peel, core and slice 1 lb (450 g) or about 3 apples. Combine in a saucepan with ⅓ cup (75 mL) water and bring to a boil. Reduce heat to a simmer, cover and cook for 20 minutes, stirring occasionally. If a smooth texture is desired, puree in a blender or food processor. This recipe makes about 1 cup (250 mL) and can easily be doubled or tripled. Store in refrigerator for up to 3 days or freeze for later use.

Head to Head: How the Nutrients Stack Up

Vegetables: Eating at least one orange and one dark green vegetable every day is recommended.

	Dark green e.g. asparagus (boiled) 125 mL	Orange e.g. carrot (raw) 125 mL	Other e.g. iceberg lettuce 250 mL
Energy (kcal)	18	28	8
Protein (g)	2	1	1
Carbohydrate (g)	3	7	2
Fibre (g)	1.6	1.4	1.2
Total Fat (g)	trace	trace	trace
Beta-carotene (mcg)	489	5113	2062
Folate (mcg)	128	26	17

Vegetables that are great sources of particular nutrients:

Fibre - lima beans, brussels sprouts, green peas, potatoes (skin on), pumpkin
Calcium - spinach, Swiss chard
Iron - asparagus, potato, spinach, Swiss chard
Vitamin A and / or beta-carotene - carrots, kale, lettuce, pumpkin, spinach, squash, sweet potato
Folate - asparagus, romaine lettuce, spinach

Week 1, Day 3

Meal	Ingredients per Serving	Canada's Food Guide Servings
Breakfast Egg 'n' Bacon Sandwiches and Apple Juice (recipe follows)	1 Egg 'n' Bacon Sandwich ¾ cup (175 mL) apple juice 1 cup (250 mL) coffee / tea 2 Tbsp (30 mL) 1% milk (optional) 1 tsp (5 mL) sugar (optional)	1 ½ Vegetables and Fruit 2 Grain Products ¾ Meat and Alternatives 1 Milk and Alternatives
Morning Snack Cottage Cheese and Fruit	½ cup (125 mL) low-fat cottage cheese ½ cup (125 mL) fruit salad in water	1 Vegetables and Fruit ½ Milk and Alternatives
Lunch Basil Chicken Salad Pita (recipe follows)	1 serving Basil Chicken Salad Pita 1 apple ½ cup (125 mL) low-fat raspberry yogurt	2 Vegetables and Fruit 2 Grain Products 1 Meat and Alternatives ½ Milk and Alternatives
Afternoon Snack Veggies and Dip with Rice Cakes	¼ cup (60 mL) zucchini rounds ¼ cup (60 mL) carrot sticks 1 Tbsp (15 mL) 1% low-fat ranch dressing 2 rice cakes	1 Vegetables and Fruit 1 Grain Products 1 Oils and Fats
Dinner Tangy Beef Stew (recipe follows)	1 serving Tangy Beef Stew 2 slices pumpernickel bread 2 tsp (10 mL) non-hydrogenated margarine 1 cup (250 mL) 1% milk	1 ¾ Vegetables and Fruit 2 Grain Products 1 Meat and Alternatives 1 Milk and Alternatives 2 Oils and Fats
Evening Snack Cinnamon Popcorn and Milk (recipe follows)	1 serving Cinnamon Popcorn 1 cup (250 mL) 1% milk	½ Grain Products 1 Milk and Alternatives
Total Servings:		7 ¼ Vegetables and Fruit 8 Grain Products 2 ¾ Meat and Alternatives 3 Milk and Alternatives 3 Oils and Fats

Good To Know

Nutrition facts of the day	Adjusting today's menu
Calories: 1843 Fat: 47 g Saturated fat: 14 g Carbohydrate: 240 g Fibre: 18 g Protein: 120 g	*To cut about 200 calories* · Skip apple juice at breakfast (saves 85 kcal) · Skip rice cakes at afternoon snack (saves 70 kcal) · Use hummus instead of margarine as spread at dinner (saves 50 kcal) *To add about 200 calories* · Spread 1 ½ tsp (7.5 mL) peanut butter on the rice cake at afternoon snack (adds 45 kcal) · Add 1 Applesauce Raisin Cookie to morning snack (adds 100 kcal) · Add 2 Tbsp (30 mL) low-fat mozzarella cheese to your chicken salad (adds 35 kcal) · Add ¼ cup (60 mL) of cinnamon popcorn at evening snack (adds 15 kcal)

Egg 'n' Bacon Sandwiches
Serves 2 - Serving Size: 1 sandwich

Ingredients:

2	eggs	2
1 tsp	1% milk	5 mL
¼ tsp	salt	1 mL
⅛ tsp	pepper	0.5 mL
1	whole-wheat English muffin, split and toasted	1
2 slices	½ oz (14 g) each back bacon	2 slices
2 Tbsp	shredded reduced-fat cheddar cheese	30 mL

Directions:

1. In a small bowl, whisk the eggs, milk, salt and pepper. Divide between two 10 oz (300 mL) microwave-safe custard cups coated with cooking spray. Microwave, uncovered, on high for 20 seconds. Stir; microwave for 20-25 seconds longer or until center of egg is almost set.

2. Place a slice of back bacon on each muffin half; top with egg and sprinkle with cheese. Microwave, uncovered, for 10-13 seconds or until cheese is melted. Let stand for 20-30 seconds before serving.

About This Recipe: You'll be surprised at how easy it is to prepare an on-the-go bacon and egg breakfast!
Per Serving: 181 kcal, 6 g fat, 2 g saturated fat, 16 g carbohydrate, 1 g fibre,14 g protein.

Healthy Tip: To make your sandwich more than ordinary, add a slice of tomato, some onions, or chopped peppers.

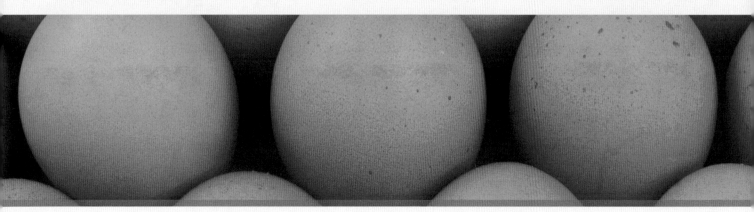

Basil Chicken Salad Pitas

Serves 4 - Serving Size: 2 pita halves, stuffed

Ingredients:

2 Tbsp	canola oil	30 mL
2 Tbsp	cider vinegar	30 mL
1	medium garlic clove, minced	1
¼ tsp	black pepper	1 mL
¼ tsp	salt	1 mL
2 cups	cooked diced chicken	500 mL
2 cups	coarsely chopped spinach	500 mL
⅓ cup	finely chopped red onion	100 mL
¼ cup	chopped fresh basil	60 mL
4	whole-wheat pita rounds, cut in half	4
8	tomato slices	8

Directions:

1. Whisk together the oil, vinegar, garlic, black pepper and salt in a medium bowl. Add the chicken, spinach, onion and basil. Toss until well coated.

2. Place a tomato slice and equal amounts of the chicken mixture in each of the pita halves.

About This Recipe: The basil adds complexity and enhances the chicken flavour of this pita dish. An easy, delicious way to use leftover chicken breast.

Per serving: 367 kcal, 11 g fat, 1.5 g saturated fat, 39 g carbohydrate, 6 g fibre, 29 g protein.

Healthy Tip: Fresh herbs like basil or mint brighten up a salad, pasta dish or meat and reduce the need for salt.

Tangy Beef Stew

Serves 5 - Serving Size: Approximately 1 cup (250 mL)

Ingredients:

2 Tbsp	all-purpose flour	30 mL
¼ tsp	salt	1 mL
⅛ tsp	pepper	0.5 mL
1 lb	stewing beef, cut into 1-inch (2.5 cm) cubes	450 g
1 ½ tsp	canola oil	7 mL
½ cup	water	125 mL
¼ cup	ketchup	60 mL
2 Tbsp	brown sugar	30 mL
2 Tbsp	vinegar	30 mL
1 ½ tsp	Worcestershire sauce	7 mL
½	large onion, chopped	½
¼	green pepper, cut in strips	¼
1 ½	carrots, sliced	1 ½
1 ½	potatoes, cubed	1 ½

Directions:

1. In bowl, combine flour, salt and pepper. Coat beef with flour mixture.

2. In large skillet, heat canola oil and brown meat on all sides.

3. In another bowl, combine water, ketchup, brown sugar, vinegar and Worcestershire sauce. Stir into browned meat. Add onion; cover. Cook over low heat for 45 minutes, stirring occasionally. Add remaining vegetables. Cook until meat and vegetables are tender, approximately 45 minutes.

 About This Recipe: This stew is sure to warm you and fill you up with good ol' fashioned nutrition from beef, carrots and potatoes.

Per serving: 293 kcal, 10 g fat, 3 g saturated fat, 23 g carbohydrate, 2 g fibre, 29 g protein.

 Cook Once, Eat Twice or More: Got leftovers? Freeze them in individual portions in freezer bags labeled and dated. Use within 2 months.

Cinnamon Popcorn
Serves 8 - Serving Size: 1 cup (250 mL)

Ingredients:

2 quarts	plain popped popcorn (about 8 cups)	2 L
1	egg white, lightly beaten	1
¼ cup	granulated sugar	60 mL
1 tsp	ground cinnamon	5 mL
¼ tsp	salt, optional	1 mL

Directions:

1. Place popcorn in a 15 x 10 inch (38 x 25 cm) baking pan.

2. In a small bowl, mix egg white, sugar, cinnamon and salt if desired. Pour over popcorn and mix thoroughly.

3. Bake at 300°C (150°F) for 20 minutes. Cool. Store in an airtight container.

 About This Recipe: Popcorn popped right is a very nutritious snack full of fibre. This simple variation keeps the calorie count low while adding some great flavour.

Per Serving: 58 kcal, 0.4 g fat, 0 g saturated fat, 13 g carbohydrate, 1 g fibre, 1 g protein.

 Healthy Tip: Use a serving of this popcorn to satisfy cravings for something sweet!

About Eggs

Choline is a nutrient required in tiny amounts for very important functions in the body. It plays a role in metabolic pathways in the liver, including those involved in synthesis of cells and their DNA, as well as brain development and nervous system function. While almost all foods contain some choline, the best dietary sources include eggs, meats, fish and whole grains.

In addition to choline, one whole egg also contains significant amounts of vitamins A, D and E, riboflavin, vitamin B_{12}, niacin and folate. Eggs also contain anti-oxidants such as lutein and omega-3 fats.

Brown and white eggs have the same nutritional value.

Week 1, Day 4

Meal	Ingredients per Serving	Canada's Food Guide Servings
Breakfast Fruit Smoothie with Toast and Peanut Butter (recipe follows)	1 serving Fruit Smoothie 1 slice whole-wheat toast 1 Tbsp (15 mL) peanut butter 1 cup (250 mL) coffee / tea 2 Tbsp (30 mL) 1% milk (optional) 1 tsp (5 mL) sugar (optional)	2 Vegetables and Fruit 1 Grain Products ½ Meat and Alternatives 1 ½ Milk and Alternatives
Morning Snack Cereal Trail Mix	½ cup (125 mL) dry multigrain Cheerios (or any dry cereal) ¼ cup (60 mL) dried fruit (apricots, banana chips, raisins, cranberries)	1 Vegetables and Fruit 1 Grain Products
Lunch Asian Cabbage Salad with Pork (recipe follows)	1 serving Asian Cabbage Salad with Pork ½ cup (125 mL) 1% milk	2 Vegetables and Fruit 1 Meat and Alternatives ½ Milk and Alternatives 1 Oils and Fats
Afternoon Snack Baked Pita with Hummus	¼ cup (60 mL) hummus ½ baked whole-wheat pita	1 Grain Products ½ Meat and Alternatives
Dinner Fish Fillets with Parsley-Cilantro Sauce, Potatoes and Asparagus (recipe follows)	1 serving Fish Fillets with Parsley-Cilantro Sauce ½ cup (125 mL) red potato 4 spears steamed asparagus ½ baked whole-wheat pita bread 1 cup (250 mL) 1% milk	1 ½ Vegetables and Fruit 1 Grain Products 2 Meat and Alternatives 1 Milk and Alternatives
Evening Snack Smart Cookie and Yogurt (recipe follows)	1 Smart Cookie ½ cup (125 mL) low-fat yogurt	1 Grain Products ¾ Milk and Alternatives
Total Servings:		6 ½ Vegetables and Fruit 5 Grain Products 4 Meat and Alternatives 3 ¾ Milk and Alternatives 1 Oils and Fats

Good To Know

Nutrition facts of the day

Calories: 1876
Fat: 53 g
Saturated fat: 13 g
Carbohydrate: 254 g
Fibre: 26 g
Protein: 109 g

Adjusting today's menu

To cut about 200 calories
· Use low-sugar jam instead of peanut butter at breakfast (saves 70 kcal)
· Replace milk with water at dinner (saves 100 kcal)
· Have ⅓ cup (75 mL) yogurt at evening snack (saves 30 kcal)

To add about 200 calories
· Mix 1 ½ Tbsp (15 mL) roasted almonds into morning snack (adds 50 kcal)
· Drink 1 cup (250 mL) of milk with your lunch (adds 100 kcal)
· For afternoon snack, increase hummus to ⅓ cup (75 mL) (adds 20 kcal)

Fruit Smoothie

Serves 2 - Serving Size: 2 cups (500 mL)

Ingredients:

2 cups	frozen unsweetened fruit mix	500 mL
1 ½ cups	low-fat vanilla yogurt	375 mL
1 cup	1% milk	250 mL
1 Tbsp	honey	15 mL

Directions:

1. Place fruit mix, yogurt, milk and honey in the blender. Blend to desired consistency. Enjoy!

About This Recipe: Experiment with your favourite fruit combinations to come up with your personalized smoothie flavour!

Per Serving: 308 kcal, 4 g fat, 2 g saturated fat, 59 g carbohydrate, 4 g fibre, 15 g protein.

Healthy Tip: For an extra healthy fibre boost, blend 2 tsp (10 mL) ground flaxseed or canola oil into your drink. To decorate, make a small fruit kabob with apple slices or a single strawberry on a toothpick to set on the brim of your glass.

Asian Cabbage Salad
Serves 4 - Serving Size: 2 cups (500 mL)

Ingredients:
Salad:

4 cups	finely shredded cabbage	1 L
2 cups	cooked diced chicken breast meat	500 mL
6 oz	snow peas or snap peas, cut in 1-inch pieces diagonally	170 g
2	green onions, sliced diagonally	2
1	jalapeno, seeds and ribs removed, thinly sliced into rounds	1
2 oz	almonds or dry roasted peanuts, toasted	55 g
½ cup	chopped fresh cilantro	125 mL
¼ cup	chopped fresh basil	60 mL

Dressing:

2 Tbsp	fresh lime juice	30 mL
1 Tbsp	white or white balsamic vinegar	15 mL
2 Tbsp	canola oil	30 mL
2 Tbsp	granulated sugar	30 mL
2 tsp	grated ginger	10 mL
½ tsp	salt	2 mL
	black pepper to taste	

Directions:

1. Place the salad ingredients in a large bowl.

2. Whisk together the salad dressing ingredients. Pour over the salad and toss until well coated. Serve immediately.

About This Recipe: A fresh side dish full of nutrients, character and MORE nutrients! Makes a great lunch. Optional mandarin orange slices add colour and vitamin C. Mix in some red cabbage for increased anti-oxidants.

Per Serving: 328 kcal, 17 g fat, 2 g saturated fat, 18 g carbohydrate, 5 g fibre, 27 g protein.

Quick Tip: Cabbage keeps better than most vegetables. Use the rest of your head of cabbage in the yummy cabbage rolls in Week 3, Day 4. Store in a plastic bag in the fridge to retain vitamin C.

Fish Fillets with Parsley-Cilantro Sauce

Serves 4 – Serving Size: 6 oz fish fillet, 2 Tbsp (30 mL) sauce

Ingredients:

1 Tbsp	canola oil	15 mL
4	6-oz (170 g) basa, tilapia or sole fillets, rinsed and patted dry	4
⅛ tsp	salt black pepper to taste	0.5 mL

Sauce:

¼ cup	chopped Italian parsley	60 mL
¼ cup	chopped fresh cilantro	60 mL
½	medium jalapeno, seeded and minced or ⅛ tsp (0.5 mL) dried pepper flakes	½
1 Tbsp	grated lemon rind	15 mL
1 Tbsp	lemon juice	15 mL
1	medium garlic clove, minced	1
1 Tbsp	canola oil	15 mL
¼ tsp	salt	1 mL

Directions:

1. Heat 1 Tbsp (15 mL) of the canola oil in a large non-stick skillet over medium-high heat. Sprinkle the fillets with ⅛ tsp of the salt and black pepper to taste. Cook for 4 minutes on each side or until fish flakes with a fork.

2. Meanwhile, combine the remaining ingredients in a small bowl. Serve fish topped with equal amounts of the sauce.

 About This Recipe: Dress up your fish with fresh herbs! That is all it needs to move into the spotlight of your dish.
Per Serving: 158 kcal, 7 g fat, 1 g saturated fat, 1 g carbohydrate, 0.3 g fibre, 24 g protein.

 Chef's Tip: When available, try fish from prairie lakes and streams, like walleye or whitefish. Save the leftover cilantro for next week, featuring Avocado Salsa (Week 2, Day 5). Cilantro is excellent for perking up any salsa.

Smart Cookies

Serves 24 - Serving Size: 1 cookie

Ingredients:

¼ cup	peanut butter	60 mL
¼ cup	margarine	60 mL
⅓ cup	brown sugar	75 mL
⅓ cup	granulated sugar	75 mL
½ tsp	vanilla	2 mL
1	egg	1
¾ cup	whole barley flour	175 mL
½ tsp	baking soda	2 mL
½ tsp	salt	2 mL
½ cup	rolled oats	125 mL
½ cup	corn flakes	125 mL
½ cup	raisins or nuts	125 mL
½ cup	chocolate chips	125 mL
1 tsp	water	5 mL

Directions:

1. In a large bowl, beat peanut butter, margarine and sugars together until smooth. Beat in vanilla and egg.

2. Add flour, soda and salt. Stir until combined. Add remaining ingredients - corn flakes, nuts and chocolate chips. Add water to help bind the dough.

3. Spoon onto a cookie sheet and bake at 375°F (190°C) for 10-12 minutes.

About This Recipe: These are the cookies to bake when you need a pick me up. Sometimes you'll bite into crunch from the corn flakes or maybe you'll find the sweetness of raisins.

Per Serving: 104 kcal, 5 g fat, 1 g saturated fat, 15 g carbohydrate, 1 g fibre, 2 g protein.

Head to Head: How the Nutrients Stack Up

Fruits: Eating a variety of fruits helps you get lots of different vitamins and minerals, plus anti-oxidants and fibre.

	Tree fruit e.g. apple – whole with skin	*Berries e.g. Raspberries – 125 mL*	*Citrus e.g. navel orange – peeled*
Energy (kcal)	72	34	62
Protein (g)	trace	1	1
Carbohydrate (g)	19	8	15
Fibre (g)	2.6	4.2	2.3
Total fat (g)	trace	trace	trace
Beta-carotene (mcg)	37	8	93
Vitamin C (mg)	6	17	70

Fruits that are great sources of particular nutrients:

Fibre - avocado, blackberries, pear with skin, prunes (cooked), raspberries
Vitamin A and / or beta-carotene - apricots, grapefruit (pink), cantaloupe
Vitamin C - kiwifruit, oranges, strawberries, rhubarb

Week 1, Day 5

Meal	Ingredients per Serving	Canada's Food Guide Servings
Breakfast Cold Cereal with Fruit	¾ cup (175 mL) bran flakes ½ cup (125 mL) strawberries 1 cup (250 mL) 1% milk 1 cup (250 mL) coffee / tea 2 Tbsp (30 mL) 1% milk (optional) 1 tsp (5 mL) sugar (optional)	1 Vegetables and Fruit 1 Grain Products 1 Milk and Alternatives
Morning Snack Apple and Peanut Butter	1 apple 2 Tbsp (30 mL) peanut butter	1 Vegetables and Fruit 1 Meat and Alternatives
Lunch Fast-fix Tomato Bean Soup with Crackers (recipe follows)	1 serving Fast-fix Tomato Bean Soup 6 whole-wheat soda crackers	3 Vegetables and Fruit ½ Grain Products 1 ½ Meat and Alternatives ½ Milk and Alternatives
Afternoon Snack Cream Cheese Tortilla Wrap	1 whole-wheat tortilla 1 oz (30 g) low-fat cream cheese ¼ cup (60 mL) bell pepper 2 ½ oz (70 g) turkey breast	½ Vegetables and Fruit 2 Grain Products 1 Meat and Alternatives 1 Oils and Fats
Dinner Coconut Ginger Shrimp with Rice (recipe follows)	1 serving Shrimp and Rice with Curry Sauce 1 cup (250 mL) 1% milk	2 Vegetables and Fruit 1 ½ Grain Products ½ Meat and Alternatives 1 Milk and Alternatives ½ Oils and Fats
Evening Snack Lentil Muffin and Fruit Salad with Yogurt Dressing (recipes follow)	1 Lentil Muffin 1 serving Fresh Fruit with Yogurt Dressing	1 Vegetables and Fruit 1 Grain Products ¼ Meat and Alternatives ½ Milk Products
Total Servings:		8 ½ Vegetables and Fruit 6 Grain Products 3 ¾ Meat and Alternatives 2 ½ Milk and Alternatives 1 ½ Oils and Fats

Good To Know

Nutrition facts of the day	Adjusting today's menu
Calories: 2215 Fat: 67 g Saturated fat: 21 g Carbohydrate: 293 g Fibre: 35 g Protein: 124 g	*To cut about 200 calories* · Spread ½ oz (15 g) cream cheese on the tortilla wrap (saves 30 kcal) · Reduce cooked rice at dinner to ½ cup (125 mL) (saves 55 kcal) · Have half of the lentil muffin instead of one (saves 95 kcal) *To add about 200 calories* · Add another ½ cup (125 mL) of milk to breakfast (adds 50 kcal) · Have ⅔ cup (150 mL) low-fat yogurt with your lunch (adds 100 kcal) · Add ¼ cup (60 mL) cooked black beans to the tortilla wrap (adds 50 kcal)

Fast-Fix Tomato Bean Soup

Serves 4 - Serving Size: 1 ½ cups (375 mL)

Ingredients:

1 Tbsp	canola oil	15 mL
1 ½ cups	diced green bell pepper	375 mL
1 cup	diced yellow onion	250 mL
2 cups	chicken broth, low-sodium	500 mL
1	medium zucchini, halved lengthwise and sliced	1
2 cups	chopped cooked chicken breast meat	500 mL
1 can	14 oz (398 mL) navy beans, rinsed and drained	1 can
¾ tsp	dried fennel seed	4 mL
2 cups	grape tomatoes, quartered or diced tomatoes	500 mL
½ cup	chopped fresh parsley	125 mL
¼ tsp	salt	1 mL
¼ cup	grated Parmesan cheese	60 mL

Directions:

1. Heat the canola oil in Dutch oven over medium-high heat. Cook the bell pepper and onion and cook for 6 minutes or until onions are richly browned on edges, stirring occasionally.

2. Add the broth, zucchini, chicken, beans and fennel. Bring to a boil over high heat. Reduce heat to medium-low, cover and cook for 12 minutes or until vegetables are tender. Add the tomatoes, parsley and salt. Remove from heat.

3. Let stand, uncovered, for 10 minutes to absorb flavours. Serve topped with cheese.

 About This Recipe: Great use of leftover chicken or turkey. One pot = rich flavour packed with protein and vitamins.
Per Serving: 370 kcal, 9 g fat, 2 g saturated fat, 39 g carbohydrate, 10 g fibre, 36 g protein.

 Healthy Tip: Add ¼ cup (125 mL) whole-wheat macaroni to make this soup a more complete meal. Make this a vegetarian meal by substituting a second type of bean for the chicken.

Coconut Ginger Shrimp with Rice

Serves 6 - Serving Size: ½ cup (125 mL) shrimp mixture

Ingredients:

1 cup	uncooked brown rice	250 mL
¼ tsp	curry powder	1 mL
1 Tbsp	canola oil	15 mL
1 cup	diced onion	250 mL
12 oz	peeled raw shrimp	340 g
1 cup	light coconut milk	250 mL
2 tsp	cornstarch	10 mL
½ cup	frozen green peas, thawed	125 mL
1 Tbsp	grated fresh ginger	15 mL
1 ½ tsp	granulated sugar	7 mL
¾ tsp	ground cumin	4 mL
¼ tsp	curry powder	1 mL
½ tsp	salt	2 mL
¼ tsp	dried pepper flakes	1 mL
¼ cup	chopped fresh cilantro	60 mL
¼ cup	chopped fresh basil	60 mL
1	medium lime, cut in four wedges	1

Directions:

1. Cook rice with ¼ tsp (1 mL) of the curry powder according to package directions, omitting any salt or fat.

2. Heat canola oil over medium heat, add the onions and cook for 5 minutes or until soft, stirring frequently. Add the shrimp and cook for an additional 3-4 minutes or until almost opaque in the centre.

3. In a small bowl, whisk together ¼ cup (60 mL) of the coconut milk and cornstarch until cornstarch is completely dissolved. Stir the coconut mixture into the skillet with the remaining coconut milk, peas, ginger, sugar, cumin, salt, pepper flakes and remaining curry powder. Increase to medium-high heat, bring to a boil and cook for 1-2 minutes or until thickened slightly. Remove from heat.

4. Spoon equal amounts of the rice in each of four shallow soup bowls or plates, spoon the shrimp mixture evenly over all, sprinkle with cilantro and basil and serve with lime wedges.

About This Recipe: This fun and exotic recipe brings together creamy coconut, spicy curry, zesty ginger and fresh cilantro sending taste buds into a tropical whirl!

Per Serving: 340 kcal, 6 g fat, 3 g saturated fat, 52 g carbohydrate, 5 g fibre, 21 g protein.

Healthy Tip: Shrimp are a good source of omega-3 fatty acids and are quick to cook when time is of the essence.

Lentil Muffins
Serves 12 - Serving Size: 1 muffin

Ingredients:

1 cup	cooked lentils (see direction 2)	250 mL
1 cup	canned apple pie filling	250 mL
1	egg	1
½ cup	canola oil	125 mL
¾ cup	whole-wheat flour	175 mL
¾ cup	all purpose flour	175 mL
⅓ cup	packed brown sugar	75 mL
2 tsp	baking powder	10 mL
1 tsp	baking soda	5 mL
1 tsp	cinnamon	5 mL
½ tsp	salt	2 mL
¼ tsp	ground allspice	1 mL
⅛ tsp	nutmeg	0.5 mL

Directions:

1. Preheat oven to 400°F (200°C). Line muffin tins with paper or silicone baking cups.

2. Prepare the lentil purée by cooking ¼ cup (60 mL) dry lentils in 1 cup (250 mL) water. When lentils are tender, purée in food processor or blender.

3. Cut apples in pie filling into small pieces.

4. Beat egg in a large mixing bowl. Stir in canola oil. Add lentil purée and apple pie filling.

5. In a separate bowl, combine flours, brown sugar, baking powder, baking soda, cinnamon, salt, allspice and nutmeg.

6. Stir dry mixture into purée mixture just until flour is moistened. Spoon batter into prepared muffin tins.

7. Bake for 15 minutes or until a toothpick inserted into centre comes out clean. Cool on wire racks.

 About This Recipe: Add some protein power to your muffins with lentils. Their flavour blends so well with the apple pie filling you won't even know you're eating a healthy muffin.

Per Serving: 232 kcal, 10 g fat, 1 g saturated fat, 33 g carbohydrate, 2 g fibre, 3 g protein.

Fruit Salad
with Yogurt Dressing

Serves 2 - Serving Size: 1 ¼ cup (300 mL)

Ingredients:

1 cup	fresh (cubed) or frozen fruits of choice	250 mL
½ cup	low-fat plain yogurt	125 mL
1 Tbsp	maple syrup	15 mL
1 Tbsp	slivered almonds	15 mL

Directions:

1. Mix together yogurt and maple syrup. Spoon over fruit.

2. Refrigerate until serving time.

3. Sprinkle with almonds just before serving. Enjoy!

About This Recipe: Simple. Nutritious. Satisfying. Try different combinations of yogurt and fruits. How about lemon or lime zest in plain yogurt with fresh raspberries?

Per Serving: 121 kcal, 3 g fat, 1 g saturated fat, 21 g carbohydrate, 2 g fibre, 5 g protein.

Healthy Tip: One ¼ cup (60 mL) serving of almonds is a source of unsaturated fats. Add some variety to the recipe by trying different nuts and seeds to top it off. This adds some different flavours and different nutrients.

Quick Tip: Cut up enough fresh fruit to last a few days. Keep refrigerated and stored in a plastic container to preserve freshness and nutrients. This makes your next fruit salad quick and easy to prepare.

Ready to Eat Substitutes

The President's Choice Blue Menu line of products was initially developed by professors in nutrition at the University of Toronto to help consumers identify ready-to-eat meals with healthy nutritional profiles. While reading product labels is the best way to identify healthy options, depending on your dietary goals, we offer these Blue Menu suggestions as substitutes for some of the recipes listed in PPEP.

Recipe	Substitute	Notes and Benefit Claims
Roasted Vegetable Penne Bake	PC Blue Menu 100% Whole-Wheat Penne with Roasted Vegetables	Single serve; Frozen; Very high in fibre
Fast-Fix Tomato Bean Soup	PC Blue Menu Hearty Vegetable and Navy Bean Soup	Tetrapack; Low-fat
Lunchbox Granola Bars	PC Blue Menu Low-fat Cranberry Apple Chewy Granola Bars	Low in Fat
Garden Dill Chicken and Rice Asparagus	PC Blue Menu Creamy Rigatoni with Chicken and Broccoli	Good source of calcium; 50% less fat than the traditionally made version.
Roasted Butternut Squash Soup	PC Blue Menu Butternut Squash Soup	Tetrapack; Low-fat
Vegetarian Chili Chowder	PC Blue Menu Vegetarian Chili	Soy protein
Minestrone with Mucho Meatballs	PC Blue Menu Minestrone Soup	Canned; Low-fat
Best Spaghetti and Meatballs	PC Blue Menu Extra Lean Italian Beef Meatballs in Tomato Sauce (just add spaghetti)	Frozen; Extra lean

Dining Out

· Ask for salad dressings and gravies 'on the side'.
· Order a salad as a starter and choose dishes that come with vegetables.
· Split a meal with your dining partner or set aside half your meal and ask to take it home. Have it the next day for lunch!
· Order an appetizer as your main course; for example, a hearty bean or meat soup paired with a whole-grain dinner roll.
· Avoid deep-fried options and rich sauces.
· Look for the Health Check symbol - some restaurants advertise healthier options this way.
· Compliment restaurant staff on their healthy menu choices and appropriate portion sizes!

Week 1, Day 6

Meal	Ingredients per Serving	Canada's Food Guide Servings
Breakfast Cinnamon French Toast and Fruit Salad with Yogurt Dressing (recipe follows)	1 serving Cinnamon French Toast 1 serving Fresh Fruit with Yogurt Dressing (Week 1, Day 5) 1 cup (250 mL) coffee / tea 2 Tbsp (30 mL) 1% milk (optional) 1 tsp (5 mL) granulated sugar (optional)	1 Vegetables and Fruit 1 Grain Products ¼ Meat and Alternatives ½ Milk and Alternatives
Morning Snack Rice Cakes with Cottage Cheese	2 rice cakes ¼ cup (60 mL) low-fat cottage cheese	1 Grain Products ¼ Milk and Alternatives
Lunch Chef's Salad (recipe follows)	1 serving Chef's Salad 2 slices pumpernickel bread 2 tsp (10 mL) margarine	3 Vegetables and Fruit 2 Grain Products 1 Meat and Alternatives ½ Milk and Alternatives 3 Oils and Fats
Afternoon Snack Graham Crackers with Peanut Butter and Orange	4 graham crackers ½ Tbsp (7 mL) peanut butter 1 orange	1 Vegetables and Fruit 1 Grain Products ¼ Meat and Alternatives
Dinner Bistro Beef Steak with Roasted Vegetables (recipe follows)	1 serving Bistro Beef Steak with Roasted Vegetables ½ cup (125 mL) green vegetables or 1 cup (250 mL) tossed salad ½ cup (125 mL) cooked brown rice 1 cup (250 mL) 1% milk	4 Vegetables and Fruit 1 Grain Products 1 ½ Meat and Alternatives 1 Milk and Alternatives
Evening Snack Betty's Gingersnap and Milk (recipe follows)	1 Betty's Gingersnap 1 cup (250 mL) 1% milk	1 Grain Products 1 Milk and Alternatives
Total Servings:		9 Vegetables and Fruit 7 Grain Products 3 Meat and Alternatives 2 ¾ Milk and Alternatives 3 Oils and Fats

Good To Know

Nutrition facts of the day	Adjusting today's menu
Calories: 2088 Fat: 81 g Saturated fat: 22g Carbohydrate: 243 g Fibre: 23 g Protein: 104 g	*To cut about 200 calories* · Skip margarine and have only 1 slice of bread at lunch (saves 150 kcal) · Skip orange at afternoon snack (saves 60 kcal) *To add about 200 calories* · Double the serving size of French toast (adds 120 kcal) · Have 8 medium baby carrots (about 80 g) with morning snack (adds 35 kcal) · Increase rice (cooked) to ¾ cup (175 mL) at dinner (adds 55 kcal)

Cinnamon French Toast

Serves 4 - Serving Size: 1 slice

Ingredients:

2	eggs	2
½ cup	1% or skim milk	125 mL
4 slices	whole-wheat bread	4 slices
½ tsp	cinnamon	2 mL

Directions:

1. Beat together eggs and milk.

2. Heat a non-stick frying pan over medium heat. Dip one slice of bread at a time into the milk mixture and coat thoroughly.

3. Place dipped bread slices in the pan. Sprinkle the top with cinnamon, to taste. Cook for 3-4 minutes, until golden brown. Flip and cook the other side.

About This Recipe: Calling all stale bread! Did you know French toast originated from a chef needing to use up leftover stale bread? What a delicious left over treat!

Per Serving: 118 kcal, 4 g fat, 1 g saturated fat, 13 g carbohydrate, 2 g fibre, 8 g protein.

Healthy Tip: Enjoy this breakfast with 1 cup (250 mL) of fresh mixed berries to start your day with a boost of vitamin C, fibre and anti-oxidants.

Chef's Salad

Serves 2 - Serving Size: Approximately 2 cups (500 mL)

Ingredients:

3 cups	spring mix salad greens	750 mL
2 slices	1 oz (30 g) each deli ham, julienned	2 slices
2 slices	1 oz (30 g) each deli turkey, julienned	2 slices
1	medium tomato, chopped	1
½ cup	sweet yellow pepper, julienned	125 mL
¼ cup	cubed cheddar cheese	60 mL
¼ cup	chopped red onion	60 mL
3 Tbsp	chopped walnuts	45 mL
2 Tbsp	dried cranberries	30 mL
2 Tbsp	sliced ripe olives	30 mL
½ tsp	Beau Monde seasoning	2 mL
¼ tsp	coarsely ground pepper	1 mL
¼ tsp	crushed red pepper flakes	1 mL
	salad dressing of your choice	

Directions:

1. In a large bowl, layer all ingredients in the order given. Serve with salad dressing of your choice.

About This Recipe: This salad has it all: Meat, veggies, nuts, fruit, cheese, and some spice! Now this is a salad that stands on its own.

Per Serving: 372 kcal, 21 g fat, 7 g saturated fat, 25 g carbohydrate, 4 g fibre, 22 g protein.

Healthy Tip: If you are watching your sodium intake, replace deli ham with a chopped hard-cooked egg (for 2 servings) and replace deli turkey with home-made turkey or chicken. You can roast a turkey or chicken breast the night before and refrigerate for quick use.

Quick Tip: Use leftover salad greens for stuffing into any type of sandwich - lots of nutrition with just a few calories!

Bistro Beef Steak with Roasted Vegetables

Serves 4 - Serving Size: 4 oz (115 g) steak

Ingredients:

1 ½ lb	new potatoes, quartered	680 g
1	red onion, cut into wedges	1
2 Tbsp	canola oil	30 mL
1 tsp	dried thyme	5 mL
	salt and pepper, to taste	
2 cups	mushrooms, halved	500 mL
1 Tbsp	canola oil	15 mL
1 lb	beef top sirloin grilling medallions or steak, 1-inch (2.5 cm) thick	450 g
2 cups	chicken broth	500 mL
2	cloves garlic, minced	2
2 Tbsp	Dijon mustard	30 mL
2 Tbsp	fresh parsley, minced	30 mL

Directions:

1. Toss potatoes and onion with 2 Tbsp (30 mL) of the canola oil, thyme and salt and pepper to taste in large roasting pan. Roast in 450°F (230°C) oven for 20 minutes. Stir in mushrooms; roast vegetables until tender, about 20 minutes.

2. Meanwhile, heat remaining canola oil in large heavy skillet over high heat. Season steak with salt and pepper to taste; cook for 5 minutes per side for medium-rare. Remove from pan; keep warm.

3. Stir broth and garlic into hot skillet; cook over medium-high heat until reduced by half, about 8 minutes. Stir in Dijon mustard and parsley. Season to taste. Toss ½ cup (125 mL) of sauce with roasted vegetables. Serve with steak and remaining sauce.

About This Recipe: These veggies are a great tasting way to dress up your steak. They add vitamins, minerals, and great flavour!

Per Serving: 459 kcal, 28 g fat, 7 g saturated fat, 20 g carbohydrate, 3 g fibre, 32 g protein.

Cook Once, Eat Twice or More: Cook up an extra-big batch of these delicious roasted vegetables and have them for lunch wrapped in a whole-wheat pita bread or tortilla.

Chef's Tip: This recipe calls for a tender cut of steak. If you prefer less tender cuts, which are generally less expensive, try a simple marinade to complement the recipe and tenderize the steak, such as ½ cup (125 mL) wine, juice of 1 lemon, 2 Tbsp (30 mL) canola oil. Marinate for 1-2 hours. Discard the marinade before cooking.

Betty's Gingersnaps
Serves 16 - Serving Size: 2 cookies

Ingredients:

½ cup	canola oil	125 mL
1 cup	granulated sugar	250 mL
1	large egg	1
¼ cup	molasses	60 mL
1 ¾ cups	all purpose flour	425 mL
2 tsp	ground ginger	10 mL
1 tsp	ground cinnamon	5 mL
1 tsp	baking powder	5 mL
1 tsp	baking soda	5 mL
½ tsp	salt	2 mL
¼ cup	granulated sugar	60 mL

Directions:

1. Preheat oven to 375°F (190°C).

2. In mixing bowl, beat canola oil with sugar. Beat in egg and molasses. Add flour, ginger, cinnamon, baking powder, baking soda and salt. Stir until dough is moist. The dough can be quite sticky.

3. Using 1 tsp (5 mL) per cookie, shape dough into ball. Roll in sugar. Place on lightly oiled baking sheet and flatten with the palm of your hand. Bake for 12-15 minutes.

4. Let cool on cookie sheets or racks.

About This Recipe: A spicy traditional treat enjoyed for centuries around the world! Treat your taste buds to a little bit of history.

Per Serving: 87 kcal; 3.3 g fat, 0.3 g saturated fat, 14 g carbohydrate, 0 fibre, 1 g protein.

Healthy Tip: Replace half the all purpose flour in this recipe with whole-wheat flour. Reduce the granulated sugar to ¾ cup (175 mL) and add a bit more spice to compensate. Freeze cookies to preserve freshness.

Substituting canola oil in a recipe that calls for solid fat, melted, is a good strategy for reducing saturated fat in baked goods. Generally, you can reduce the fat content by 20-25% in any recipe that calls for more than ¼ cup (60 mL) fat by substituting oil for solid fat.

Example: Instead of 1 cup (250 mL) of solid fat (melted), use ¾ cup (175 mL) canola oil. Note that this method works well for most baked goods, but for certain products requiring solid fat (shortbread, for example) this will not work well.

Growing Fruit on the Prairies

In times past, nearly every prairie yard had a raspberry patch and an abundance of rhubarb. Saskatoon berries were plentiful in every ravine and river valley but most tree fruits weren't hardy enough to withstand the winters. Breeding programs such as the one at the University of Saskatchewan have increased the variety of cold-hardy fruit trees and shrubs available for prairie gardeners and commercial growers. U-Pick operations in every province offer the opportunity for a family outing during the harvest season.

Prairie gardeners can grow a variety of hardy dwarf sour cherries and apples. Among the apple varieties some, such as the Wealthy, were known to the pioneers who prized them for both eating and cooking. Others, like the aptly named Prairie Sun and Prairie Sensation have been developed in recent years.

Strawberries and raspberries grow well on the prairies. In addition, many Saskatoon varieties are available for backyard gardeners. A new crop is the Haskap or honeyberry, which tastes something like a blueberry and grows on a shrub suitable in size for an urban backyard (Note that two plants are required for pollination). Rhubarb (which is actually a vegetable) is still a favourite with many people, being among the first crops ready for harvest in early summer and delicious baked into pies, breads and crisps.

Researchers at the University of Alberta have studied the nutritional characteristics of Saskatoon berries. The dark blue-red colour of Saskatoons is due to high amounts of anti-oxidant compounds in the skin and flesh. According to the United States Department of Agriculture, Saskatoon berries have the most anti-oxidant activity in a list of 40 fruits and vegetables. This activity is found in flavonoid compounds that give Saskatoons their deep purple colour. The types and amounts of flavonoids present have been characterized by researchers at the University of Alberta. Saskatoons are also a good source of fibre and iron.

Week 1, Day 7

Meal	Ingredients per Serving	Canada's Food Guide Servings
Breakfast Berry Wheat Germ Pancakes with Bacon (recipe follows)	1 serving Berry Wheat Germ Pancakes 1 slice back bacon 1 tsp (5 mL) non-hydrogenated margarine 1 Tbsp (15 mL) maple syrup ½ cup (125 mL) red grapes 1 cup (250 mL) coffee / tea 2 Tbsp (30 mL) 1% milk (optional) 1 tsp (5 mL) granulated sugar (optional)	1 ½ Vegetables and Fruit 1 Grain Products ½ Meat and Alternatives ¼ Milk and Alternatives 1 Oils and Fats
Morning Snack Lunchbox Granola Bar and Banana (recipe follows)	1 Lunchbox Granola Bar 1 banana	1 Vegetables and Fruit 1 Grain Products
Lunch Barley with Caramelized Vegetables (recipe follows)	1 serving Barley with Caramelized Vegetables ½ whole-wheat pita 2 Tbsp (30 mL) salsa 1 cup (250 mL) 1% milk	1 ½ Vegetables and Fruit 2 Grain Products 1 Milk and Alternatives 1 Oils and Fats
Afternoon Snack Pizza Bagel	½ whole-wheat bagel 2 Tbsp (30 mL) salsa ¾ oz (22 g) low-fat mozzarella cheese Green pepper and olives (optional)	1 Grain Products ½ Milk and Alternatives
Dinner Garden Dill Chicken and Rice Asparagus (recipes follow)	1 serving Garden Dill Chicken and Rice Asparagus	1 ½ Vegetables and Fruit 2 Grain Products 1 Meat and Alternatives
Evening Snack Canned Peaches with Frozen Yogurt Bar	½ cup (125 mL) canned peaches (in water) 1 Chapman's® vanilla frozen yogurt bar	1 Vegetables and Fruit 1 Milk and Alternatives
Total Servings:		6 ½ Vegetables and Fruit 6 ½ Grain Products 1 ½ Meat and Alternatives 2 ¾ Milk and Alternatives 2 Oils and Fats

Good To Know

Nutrition facts of the day	Adjusting today's menu
Calories: 1794 Fat: 43 g Saturated fat: 11 g Carbohydrate: 266 g Fibre: 31 g Protein: 94 g	*To cut about 200 calories* · Have only 1 pancake at breakfast (saves 100 kcal) · Have only ¾ serving of Garden Dill Chicken and Rice Asparagus (saves 100 kcal) · Omit the raisins in the Lunchbox Granola Bars (saves 20 kcal) *To add about 200 calories* · Drink ½ cup (125 mL) 1% milk with your breakfast (adds 50 kcal) · Have 1 Tbsp (15 mL) peanut butter with banana at morning snack (adds 90 kcal) · At lunch, instead of a pita, have 2 slices of whole-wheat toast (adds 60 kcal)

Berry Wheat Germ Pancakes

Serves 3 - Serving Size: 2 pancakes

Ingredients:

⅔ cup	low-fat milk	150 mL
1	medium egg, lightly beaten	1
½ tsp	vanilla	2 mL
2 tsp	canola oil	10 mL
½ cup	whole-wheat flour	125 mL
2 Tbsp	wheat germ	30 mL
1 Tbsp	ground flaxseed	15 mL
⅛ tsp	salt	0.5 mL
1 ½ tsp	baking powder	7.5 mL
½ cup	frozen-thawed or fresh Saskatoons or blueberries	125 ml

Directions:

1. In a measuring cup, combine milk, eggs, vanilla and canola oil.

2. In a mixing bowl, combine flour, wheat germ, flaxseed, salt, and baking powder.

3. Add wet to dry ingredients in the mixing bowl. Stir until just combined. Add berries and stir.

4. Heat a non-stick skillet over medium heat. Add about ¼ cup (60 mL) of the batter to the hot pan for each pancake. When bubbles appear on the surface of the batter, flip and continue to cook until golden brown.

 About This Recipe: The addition of wheat germ and fruit to this pancake boosts the amount of fibre, vitamins and minerals. This flapjack just went from ordinary to extraordinary!

Per Serving: 190 kcal, 6 g fat, 1 g saturated fat, 26 g carbohydrate, 5 g fibre, 9 g protein.

 Healthy Tip: Wheat germ is the reproductive part of the plant that is commonly removed with the bran layer when wheat grains are processed or refined. 1 Tbsp (15 mL) of wheat germ contains 27 kcal, 0.6 g unsaturated fat, 3.5 g carbohydrate, 1.1 g fibre and 2.2 g protein. It is also a source of folate.

Lunchbox Granola Bars

Serves 24 - Serving Size: 1 bar

Ingredients:

2 cups	rolled oats	500 mL
1 cup	whole-wheat flour	250 mL
½ cup	ground flaxseed	125 mL
2 Tbsp	packed brown sugar	30 mL
1 tsp	cinnamon	5 mL
½ cup	sunflower seeds	125 mL
½ tsp	salt	2 mL
¾ cup	raisins, chocolate chips or favourite dried fruit	175 mL
⅓ cup	honey	75 mL
1	large egg, beaten	1
¼ cup	canola oil	60 mL
¼ cup	applesauce	60 mL
2 tsp	vanilla	10 mL

Directions:

1. Preheat oven to 350°F (180°C). Grease a 9 x 13 inch (22 x 33 cm) baking pan.

2. In a large bowl, mix together the oats, flour, flaxseed, brown sugar, cinnamon, raisins, sunflower seeds and salt. Make a well in the centre and set aside.

3. In a small bowl, combine honey, egg, canola oil, applesauce and vanilla. Add liquid ingredients, raisins, chocolate chips or favourite fruit to the well with the dry ingredients and mix. Pat the mixture evenly into the prepared pan.

4. Bake for 20-25 minutes in the preheated oven, until bars begin to turn golden at the edges.

5. Cool for 5 minutes, then cut into bars while still warm. Do not allow the bars to cool completely before cutting, or they will be too hard to cut.

About This Recipe: What a tasty way to get your fibre and vitamins for the day! This is a great snack to grab on the go that will keep you full until your next meal.

Per Serving: 131 kcal, 5 g fat, 0.4 g saturated fat, 20 g carbohydrate, 3 g fibre, 3 g protein.

Barley with Caramelized Vegetables

Serves 8 - Serving Size: Approximately 1 cup (250 mL)

Ingredients:

1	canola oil	1
1 Tbsp	medium onion, thinly sliced	15 mL
1 cup	pearl barley	250 mL
4 cups	low-sodium vegetable broth	1 L
1 Tbsp	canola oil	15 mL
1	red pepper, thinly sliced	1
3 cups	sliced mushrooms	750 mL
1	garlic clove, finely chopped	1
1	zucchini, cut into thin strips	1
3 Tbsp	balsamic vinegar	45 mL
1 Tbsp	brown sugar	15 mL

Directions:

1. In a saucepan, heat first amount of canola oil over medium-high. Add barley and toast for 3-4 minutes. Add broth to barley. Bring to a boil, then reduce heat and simmer, uncovered, until barley is tender, for about 40-45 minutes.

2. Drain off excess broth and cover to keep barley warm.

3. Meanwhile, in a large frying pan, heat second amount of canola oil. Add onion and sauté for about 5 minutes, stirring frequently. Add red pepper, mushrooms and garlic. Sauté for 3-4 minutes. Add zucchini, balsamic vinegar and brown sugar and continue to cook for about 4-5 minutes longer. Season with pepper. Serve over barley.

 About This Recipe: Caramelized vegetables are a great way to convert those non veggie lovers to the world of nutritious veggies. They can be sweet and delicious. Really!

Per Serving: 161 kcal, 4 g fat, 0.3 g saturated fat, 28 g carbohydrate, 5 g fibre, 4 g protein.

 Healthy Tip: Barley in combination with a variety of vegetables makes this recipe a high source of fibre and an excellent source of vitamin C.

 Quick Tip: Vegetable dishes are a great way to use up bits and pieces of various veggies and save money. Go through your produce drawers and use up anything you don't have in the menu plan for the rest of the week.

Garden Dill Chicken and Rice Asparagus

Serves 4 - Serving Size: 1 ¼ cups (300 mL)

Ingredients:

24	about 1 lb (450 g) asparagus spears, ends trimmed	24
3 cups	water	750 mL
¼ tsp	salt	1 mL
1 cup	uncooked brown rice	250 mL
¼ tsp	ground turmeric (or curry powder)	1 mL
3	medium green onions, finely chopped, divided	3
2 cups	chicken breast meat, cooked, diced	500 mL
1 oz	Swiss cheese (grated), torn into smaller pieces	30 g
3 Tbsp	fresh dill, chopped	45 mL
2 Tbsp	canola oil	30 mL
½ tsp	salt	2 mL
¼ tsp	black pepper	1 mL

Directions:

1. Bring water to a boil in a large non-stick skillet over medium-high heat. Add the asparagus and ¼ tsp (1 mL) of the salt. Cover and cook for 2-3 minutes or until just tender crisp. Remove asparagus from skillet and set aside on separate plate.

2. Add the rice, turmeric and half of the onions to the asparagus water. Bring to a boil over medium-high heat, reduce heat to low, cover and cook for 40 minutes or until rice is done and water has been absorbed.

3. Remove from heat, stir in the chicken, cheese, dill, canola oil, salt and black pepper. Cover and let stand for 5 minutes to heat through.

4. Serve rice mixture as bed for the asparagus and sprinkle with the remaining green onions.

 About This Recipe: The fresh dill brings this chicken recipe to a new level of freshness, while the Swiss cheese brings its own tang and added calcium.

Per Serving: 404 kcal, 13 g fat, 3 g saturated fat, 42 g carbohydrate, 4 g fibre, 30 g protein.

Cheese belongs to the Milk and Alternatives food group in *Eating Well with Canada's Food Guide*. One serving of hard cheese (such as swiss) is 1 ½ oz (50 g). People living in the Prairies eat 7-8 kg of cheese per year, according to the Dairy Farmers of Canada. Canadians' favourite cheeses are mozzarella and cheddar but if you're looking for something different, check out some of the Prairies' local cheese producers, currently found mainly in Alberta. Consult a specialty cheese shop, go on a farm tour, or search the Internet. Everything from harvarti to feta to gouda, made from cow, sheep or goat's milk is locally available.

Sources of Week 1 Recipes - From the PANDA Nutrition Team

Breakfast Parfait
Roasted Apple Pork Tenderloin *(developed by Nancy Hughes)*
Basic Grilled Chicken
Basil Chicken Salad Pitas *(developed by Nancy Hughes)*
Fruit Smoothie
Asian Cabbage Salad *(developed by Nancy Hughes)*
Fish Fillets with Fresh Parsley-Cilantro Sauce *(developed by Nancy Hughes)*
Fast-Fix Tomato Bean Soup *(developed by Nancy Hughes)*
Coconut Ginger Shrimp with Rice *(developed by Nancy Hughes)*
Fruit Salad with Yogurt Dressing
Cinnamon French Toast
Berry Wheat Germ Pancakes
Garden Dill Chicken and Rice Asparagus *(developed by Nancy Hughes)*

Used with Permission

Alberta Milk: Fresh Raspberry Muffins
Taste of Home: Tuna Caesar Sandwiches, Egg 'n' Bacon Sandwiches, Cinnamon Popcorn, Chef's Salad, Roasted Vegetable Penne Bake
Progressive Foods Inc.: Quick Cooking Barley Breakfast Delight
Alberta Barley Commission: Applesauce Raisin Cookies, Smart Cookies
CanolaInfo.org: Tangy Beef Stew, Betty's Gingersnaps, Lunchbox Granola Bars, Barley with Carmelized Vegetables
Alberta Pulse Growers Commission: Lentil Muffins, Five-Minute Hummus
Canada Beef: Bistro Beef Steak with Roasted Vegetables

For more recipes visit: www.pureprairie.ca

Average Intakes of Week 1:

By Food Group:	By Nutrient Profile:
8 Vegetables and Fruit servings 7 Grains servings 3 Meat and Alternatives servings 3 Milk and Alternatives servings	Total energy: 1985 kcal 59 g Fat (27% of total energy) 15 g Saturated Fat (7% of total energy) 264 g Carbohydrate (53% of total energy) 30 g Fibre 110 g Protein (20% of total energy)

Grocery List Week 2

Food Group	Food Item	
Vegetables & Fruit	Apples*†	Mushrooms*†
	Avocado	Onions, yellow / red*†
	Bananas†	Orange juice, fresh or from concentrate
	Basil, fresh*†	Parsley, fresh*†
	Beets, fresh or canned*	Parsnip*
	Blueberries or Saskatoons, fresh / frozen*†	Peas, snap*†
	Butternut squash*	Peppers, chili / jalapeno*†
	Carrots*†	Peppers, sweet, green*†
	Celery	Potatoes*†
	Cilantro, fresh*†	Radishes*
	Corn kernels, fresh or canned*	Romaine lettuce / Salad greens / Spring Mix*
	Cucumber*†	Spinach*†
	Fennel bulb	Strawberries*
	Garlic*†	Tomatoes, Roma / grape*†
	Grapefruit	Zucchini*†
	Grapes, red†	
	Green beans*	
	Green chilies	
	Green onion*†	
	Kale*	
	Kiwifruit	
	Leeks*	
	Lemons†	
	Limes†	
	Mandarin oranges	
	Mint, fresh*	
Grain Products	All-bran bar	
	Bagel, whole-wheat*†	
	Bread, raisin and whole-wheat*†	
	Bread, pumpernickel*†	
	English muffin, whole-wheat*†	
	Pita bread, whole-wheat*†	
	Shreddies, or similar cereal	
	Tortillas, whole-wheat / corn*†	
Milk & Alternatives	Buttermilk, low-fat*	
	Cheddar cheese, low-fat*†	
	Feta cheese*	
	Milk, 1% M.F. or skim*†	
	Milk, 1% M.F., chocolate*	
	Mozzarella cheese, low-fat*†	
	Sour cream, low-fat*	
	Yogurt, low-fat, Greek-style	
	Yogurt, low-fat, vanilla / strawberry*†	
Meat & Alternatives	Bacon bits	
	Beef, sirloin or strip loin*†	
	Chicken breast, boneless, skinless*†	
	Eggs*†	
	Fish fillets*	
	Ground beef, lean*†	
	Tuna, canned in water	
	Turkey breast, sliced*	

Prairie-produced foods.
† Foods also listed in week 1

Week 2, Day 1

Meal	Ingredients per Serving	Canada's Food Guide Servings
Breakfast Breakfast Bar with Yogurt and Fruit	¾ cup (175 mL) low-fat strawberry yogurt 1 apple 1 All-Bran Bar 1 cup (250 mL) coffee / tea 2 Tbsp (30 mL) 1% milk (optional) 1 tsp (5 mL) granulated sugar (optional)	1 Vegetables and Fruit 1 Grain Products 1 Milk and Alternatives
Morning Snack Baked Biscuit and Banana (recipe follows)	1 Baked Biscuit 1 banana	1 Grain Products 1 Vegetables and Fruit
Lunch Black Bean Burger (recipe follows)	1 Black Bean Burger 1 cup (250 mL) chopped romaine lettuce 1 Tbsp (15 mL) low-fat salad dressing	2 Vegetables and Fruit 2 Grain Products 1 Meat and Alternatives 1 Oils and Fats
Afternoon Snack Nuts, Seeds and Crunch Mix (recipe follows)	1 serving Nuts, Seeds and Crunch Mix	1 Grain Products ½ Meat and Alternatives
Dinner Dijon Beef and Greens with Yam "Fries" (recipes follow)	1 serving Dijon Beef and Greens 1 serving Yam "Fries" 1 slice whole-wheat toast ½ cup (125 mL) 1% milk	3 ½ Vegetables and Fruit 1 Grain Products 1 ½ Meat and Alternatives ½ Milk and Alternatives 1 ½ Oils and Fats
Evening Snack Fresh Raspberry Muffin and Yogurt (see week 1)	1 Fresh Raspberry Muffin ¾ cup (175 mL) low-fat yogurt	1 Grain Products 1 Milk and Alternatives
Total Servings:		7 Vegetables and Fruit 7 Grain Products 3 Meat and Alternatives 2 ½ Milk and Alternatives 2 ½ Oils and Fats

Good To Know

Nutrition facts of the day	Adjusting today's menu
Calories: 2038 Fat: 56 g Saturated fat: 14 g Carbohydrate: 297 g Fibre: 43 g Protein: 100 g	*To cut about 200 calories* · Reduce yogurt to ½ cup (125 mL) at breakfast (saves 50 kcal) · Skip banana at morning snack (saves 50 kcal) · Cut the serving size of the afternoon snack in half (saves 100 kcal) *To add about 200 calories* · Have 1 Tbsp (15 mL) peanut butter with your morning snack (adds 90 kcal) · Add 1 cup (250 mL) of low-fat milk to lunch (adds 100 kcal)

Baked Biscuits
Serves 15 - Serving Size: 1 biscuit

Ingredients:

1 ¾ cup	all-purpose flour	425 mL
1 Tbsp	baking powder	15 mL
1 Tbsp	granulated sugar	15 mL
Dash	salt	Dash
¼ cup	unsalted non-hydrogenated margarine or butter	60 mL
⅔ cup	lentil purée (see Quick Tip)	150 mL
⅔ cup	1% milk	150 mL

Directions:

1. Preheat oven to 425ºF (220ºC).

2. In a large mixing bowl, combine flour, baking powder, sugar and salt.

3. Cut margarine into mixture and add lentil purée (still cutting) until it resembles coarse oatmeal.

4. Add milk and fold into flour mixture until ingredients are just incorporated.

5. Turn out dough onto a lightly floured surface and pat down to 1 ½-2-inches (4-5 cm) thick. Cut out biscuits with a 2-inch (5 cm) cookie cutter or round glass. Dust cookie cutter with flour to help prevent dough from sticking.

6. Place biscuits on baking sheet at least 1-inch (2.5 cm) apart. Bake for 14-16 minutes, or until golden. Serve immediately.

About This Recipe: This biscuit has some added protein pizzazz from the lentil purée! An easy way to add fibre and vitamins to a simple staple food.

Per Serving: 102 kcal, 3 g fat, 0.5 g saturated fat, 15 g carbohydrate, 1 g fibre, 3 g protein.

Quick Tip: To purée pulses, place cooked or rinsed and drained canned pulses into a food processor, add ¼ cup (60 mL) hot water for every 1 cup (250 mL) of cooked pulses, and purée until the mixture is smooth, adding more water in small amounts to reach desired consistency, similar to baby food, for about 5 minutes. Scrape the bowl as needed. Unused purée can be frozen and kept for several months in the freezer.

Canada is one of the leading producers of pulse crops, such as lentils. Saskatchewan growers produce 97% of Canada's lentil crop. Studies suggest that eating lentils and other pulse grains such as dried beans reduces the rise in blood sugar after a meal. A study of the literature conducted by researchers at the University of Toronto found that this effect was consistent for people with normal blood sugar and those with type 2 diabetes.

Black Bean Burgers

Serves 4 - Serving Size: 1 burger

Ingredients:

1 can	**19 oz (540 mL) black beans, drained and rinsed**	1 can
1 cup	**cooked brown rice**	250 mL
1	**small onion, chopped**	1
2	**green onions, finely chopped**	2
½ tsp	**Tabasco sauce, optional**	2 mL
1	**large egg**	1
¼ cup	**whole-wheat bread crumbs**	60 mL
2 Tbsp	**salsa**	30 mL
4	**hamburger buns**	4
¼ cup	**low-fat plain yogurt**	60 mL
4 Tbsp	**salsa**	60 mL
4	**romaine lettuce leaves**	4
1	**avocado, sliced, optional**	1

Directions:

1. Preheat oven to 350ºF (180ºC).

2. In a large bowl, coarsely mash beans with a potato masher or fork.

3. Add rice, onions, Tabasco sauce if desired, egg, bread crumbs and 2 Tbsp of salsa. Mix well.

4. Divide mixture into four and form into patties that are about 1-inch (2.5 cm) thick.

5. Cook over medium heat on a non-stick pan for 4-5 minutes each side or until lightly browned.

6. Transfer to a pan and cook in preheated oven for 10 minutes.

7. In a small bowl, combine remaining salsa and yogurt. Serve with lettuce and avocado (if desired) as a condiment to your burger.

 About This Recipe: A great tasting vegetarian alternative that is truly filling!
Per Serving: 451 kcal, 12 g fat, 2 g saturated fat, 71 g carbohydrate, 19 g fibre, 19 g protein.

 Healthy Tip: The black beans, brown rice and vegetables makes this lunch a high source of fibre (15 g per serving!). Black beans by themselves also provide 30% of your daily requirement for folate.

Nuts, Seeds and Crunch Mix

Serves 16 - Serving Size: ½ cup (125 mL)

Ingredients:

4 cups	whole-wheat shreddies-style cereal	1 L
¾ cup	chopped walnuts	175 mL
¾ cup	pretzels, broken into smaller pieces	175 mL
¾ cup	hulled pumpkin seeds	175 mL
2 Tbsp	canola oil	30 mL
2 Tbsp	prepared mustard	30 mL
2 Tbsp	Worcestershire sauce	30 mL
2 tsp	curry powder	10 mL
1 tsp	ground cumin	5 mL
⅛ tsp	cayenne (optional)	0.5 mL
1 tsp	salt	5 mL
2 Tbsp	grated fresh lemon zest	30 mL

Directions:

1. Preheat the oven to 300°F (150°C).

2. Combine the cereal, walnuts, pretzels and pumpkin seeds in a large bowl.

3. Whisk together the remaining ingredients, except the lemon rind, in a small bowl. Pour over the cereal mixture and toss until well blended. Place in a thin layer on two large baking sheets and bake for 7 minutes, stir and bake for an additional 6 minutes or until just beginning to lightly brown. (Note: The mixture will continue to darken in color and cook slightly after being removed from the oven.)

4. Remove from oven, stir in the zest. Let stand for at least 30 minutes to absorb flavours.

 About This Recipe: This fun and easy munchie mix ensures you get some of those important vitamins and minerals for the day and it satisfies your hunger!

Per Serving: 184 kcal, 10 g fat, 1 g saturated fat, 21 g carbohydrate, 3 g fibre, 6 g protein.

 Healthy Tip: A serving of this recipe is a source of protein and fibre but this is an energy-dense snack (184 kcal per half-cup) so adjust the serving size according to your energy needs. Take some to work and share with your co-workers.

 Chef's Tip: For a crispier, more flavourful snack, let stand 2 hours before serving. Store leftovers in an airtight container for up to 2 weeks.

Dijon Beef and Greens

Serves 4 - Serving Size: 4 oz (115 g) steak

Ingredients:

1 lb	lean sirloin or strip loin steak	450 g
2 Tbsp	Dijon mustard	30 mL
½ tsp	cracked pepper	2 mL
1 Tbsp	Dijon mustard	15 mL
2 Tbsp	red wine vinegar	30 mL
2 Tbsp	fat-free mayonnaise	30 mL
½ tsp	sugar	2 mL
½ tsp	crushed garlic	2 mL
1	10 oz (280 g) package mixed salad greens	1

Directions:

1. Reserve 2 Tbsp (30 mL) mustard. Spread remainder on steak and top with pepper. Broil or grill steaks for about 5 minutes per side for medium.

2. Meanwhile, in a small mixing bowl whisk together reserved mustard, vinegar, mayonnaise, sugar and garlic. Toss greens with dressing, reserving 2 Tbsp (30 mL) dressing for topping.

3. Divide greens onto serving plates. Slice steaks into thin strips, place on greens and drizzle with reserved dressing.

About This Recipe: Only 8 ingredients! Super simple and looks deluxe when plated with the salad greens. Serve with Yam Fries.

Per Serving: 251 kcal, 8 g fat, 3 g saturated fat, 9 g carbohydrate, 2 g fibre, 34 g protein.

Quick Tip: You can also make a wrap with this recipe.

Yam "Fries"
with Cajun Dipping Sauce

Serves 6 - Serving Size: ½ cup (125 mL)

Ingredients:

1 ½ lb	yams	675 g
2 Tbsp	canola oil	30 mL
1 tsp	smoked paprika	5 mL
½ tsp	coarsely ground black pepper	2 mL

Cajun dipping sauce:

¾ cup	fat-free sour cream	175 mL
1 Tbsp	Louisiana hot sauce or Tabasco sauce	15 mL
1	medium garlic clove, minced	1

Directions:

1. Preheat oven to 450°F (230°C). Line large 11 x 17 inch (28 x 43 cm) baking sheet with aluminum foil.

2. Peel yams and cut in half lengthwise. Then slice into ½-inch (1 cm) slices, and finally into 1-inch (2.5 cm) strips, to resemble fries.

3. Place yams in large bowl. Drizzle canola oil over potatoes and toss gently, yet thoroughly to coat. Sprinkle with paprika and black pepper and toss gently.

4. Arrange yams in single layer on baking sheet. Bake for 30-35 minutes, turning with a spatula after 20 minutes, or until beginning to brown.

5. Serve immediately for peak flavour and texture.

 About This Recipe: This crowd pleasing recipe full of vitamin A is sure to become a quick classic. Sweet and satisfying!
Per Serving: 159 kcal, 5 g fat, 0.6 g saturated fat, 25 g carbohydrates, 3 g fibre, 3 g protein.

 Healthy Tip: Yams are a good source fibre and potassium. If you want an extra boost of beta-carotene and a lower glycemic index (see page 87) use sweet potatoes instead of yams.

 Quick Tip: Try other spices with your fries such as cumin and chili powder or a sprinkle of cinnamon for a different taste.

Head to Head: How the Nutrients Stack Up

Grain Products - Breads: Choose whole grain breads to triple the fibre.

	White, commercial – 1 slice	Whole-wheat, commercial – 1 slice	Pumpernickel – 1 slice
Energy (kcal)	93	86	88
Protein (g)	3	3	3
Carbohydrate (g)	18	16	17
Fibre (g)	0.8	2.4	2.3
Total fat (g)	1	1	1
Sodium	238	184	235
Folate*	60	18	47

*In Canada, white flour is fortified with folate while whole grain flours are natural sources.

Grain Products - Other: These grains have similar nutrient profiles, but whole-wheat pastas and barley are higher in fibre. In fact, barley fibre helps to lower cholesterol, which is a risk factor for heart disease.

	Rice, brown long-grain, cooked – 125 mL	Spaghetti, whole-wheat, cooked – 125 mL	Barley, pearled cooked – 125 mL
Energy (kcal)	115	92	102
Protein (g)	3	4	2
Carbohydrate (g)	24	20	23
Fibre (g)	1.5	2.4	2.0
Total fat (g)	1	0.5	trace

Week 2, Day 2

Meal	Ingredients per Serving	Canada's Food Guide Servings
Breakfast Whole-wheat Toast with Peanut Butter and Orange	1 slice whole-wheat toast 1 Tbsp (15 mL) peanut butter 1 mandarin orange 1 cup (250 mL) coffee / tea 2 Tbsp (30 mL) 1% milk (optional) 1 tsp (5 mL) granulated sugar (optional)	1 Vegetables and Fruit 1 Grain Products ½ Meat and Alternatives
Morning Snack Smart Cookie and Milk (see week 1)	1 Smart Cookie 1 cup (250 mL) 1% milk	1 Grain Products 1 Milk and Alternatives
Lunch Roasted Butternut Squash Soup with Greens and Beet Salad (recipes follow)	1 serving Roasted Butternut Squash Soup 1 serving Greens and Beet Salad 6 whole-wheat soda crackers	4 ½ Vegetables and Fruit 1 Grain Products ½ Milk and Alternatives 2 Oils and Fats
Afternoon Snack Tuna and Crackers	½ cup (125 mL) cranberry juice 6 Melba toast 2 ½ oz (70 g) tuna	1 Vegetables and Fruit 1 ½ Grain Products 1 Meat and Alternatives
Dinner Barbecue Chicken Pita Pizza (recipe follows)	1 serving Barbecue Chicken Pita Pizza 1 cup (250 mL) shredded romaine lettuce ¼ cup (60 mL) each sliced cucumber and carrots 1 Tbsp (15 mL) salad dressing of choice	2 Vegetables and Fruit 2 Grain Products ½ Meat and Alternatives ½ Milk and Alternatives 2 Oils and Fats
Evening Snack Cookie Crumble Baked Apple (recipe follows)	1 serving Cookie Crumble Baked Apple 1 cup (250 mL) 1% milk	1 Vegetables and Fruit 1 Grain Product 1 Milk and Alternatives
Total Servings:		9 ½ Vegetables and Fruit 7 ½ Grain Products 2 Meat and Alternatives 3 Milk and Alternatives 3 Oils and Fats

Good To Know

Nutrition facts of the day	Adjusting today's menu
Calories: 1987 Fat: 57 g Saturated fat: 12 g Carbohydrate: 287 g Fibre: 32 g Protein: 95 g	*To cut about 200 calories* · Reduce milk to ½ cup (125 mL) at morning snack (saves 50 kcal) · Have an apple at evening snack without any preparation (saves 50 kcal) · Use only 1 Tbsp (15 mL) dressing on salad at lunch (saves 100 kcal) *To add about 200 calories* · Add a slice of whole-wheat toast to breakfast (adds 70 kcal) · Add ¾ oz (23 g) low-fat cheddar cheese to afternoon snack (adds 35 kcal) · Double the amount of chicken to ½ cup (125 mL) for the barbecue pizza (adds 50 kcal) · Add 1 Tbsp (15 mL) of sunflower seeds to evening snack (adds 50 kcal)

Roasted Butternut Squash Soup

Serves 4-5 - Serving Size: Approximately 2 cups (500 mL)

Ingredients:

3 cups	butternut squash, peeled and cubed	750 mL
½	medium onion, peeled	½
½	large parsnip, peeled, cut in half	½
½	head garlic	½
1 Tbsp	canola oil, divided	15 mL
½	large Granny Smith apple, cored	½
3 cups	chicken or vegetable broth, low-sodium	750 mL
½ tsp	fennel seed, optional	2 mL
⅜ tsp	Italian seasoning	1.5 mL
¼ tsp	cinnamon	1 mL
⅛ tsp	nutmeg	0.5 mL
1 tsp	Mrs. Dash Original Seasoning	5 mL
1	bay leaf	1
1 cup	low-fat Greek yogurt	250 mL
2 Tbsp	1% milk	30 mL
1 ½ tsp	cornstarch	7 mL
2 Tbsp	chopped parsley	30 mL
	salt and pepper, to taste	

Directions:

1. Preheat oven to 350°F (175°C). Line a baking sheet with parchment paper or foil.
2. In a large bowl toss squash, onion and parsnip in 1 ½ tsp (7 mL) of the canola oil and place on baking sheet.
3. Slice top of the head of garlic and brush with canola oil. Wrap garlic in foil and set on baking sheet with vegetables.

4. Place baking sheet in oven and roast for 45-50 minutes until vegetables are fork tender. Remove baking sheet from oven. Set garlic aside. While vegetables are roasting, lightly brush apple with remaining 1 ½ tsp (7 mL) canola oil and add to pan the last 15 minutes of roasting.

5. In a medium pot on low heat, add broth, fennel seed, Italian seasoning, cinnamon, nutmeg and Mrs. Dash. Stir well. Squeeze garlic cloves out of their skin into a food processor or large blender. In batches, add roasted vegetables and apples, adding just enough broth to blend until smooth. Transfer pureed soup to a large pot. Repeat until all vegetables and broth are pureed. Add bay leaf and bring to a gentle simmer for 10-15 minutes and reduce to low heat.

6. In medium bowl, mix ¾ cup (175 mL) of Greek yogurt, milk and cornstarch. Stir well to blend thoroughly. Slowly add about 1 cup (250 mL) of soup to the yogurt mixture, stirring well. Return mixture to soup pot and stir, add salt and pepper to taste and simmer gently for 5-10 minutes.

7. Mix parsley with remaining yogurt and refrigerate until ready to serve. Ladle soup into a bowl and garnish with a dollop of the yogurt mixture.

About This Recipe: A sweet and savoury soup to enjoy on a nippy day. A comforting way to fill up on your vitamins. Serve with Greens and Beet Salad.

Per Serving: 223 kcal, 5 g fat, 1 g saturated fat, 37 g carbohydrate, 8 g fibre, 11 g protein.

Greens and Beet Salad
with Honey Balsamic Dressing
Serves 4 - Serving Size: 2 cups salad (500 mL)

Ingredients:

6 cups	fresh spinach leaves	1.5 L
½ cup	thinly sliced red onion	125 mL
6 oz	fresh beets, (about 2 medium) peeled, very thinly sliced and cut in half or 1 10 oz (284 mL) canned sliced beets, drained and cut in half	170 g
¼ cup	slivered almonds, toasted	60 mL

Dressing:

3 Tbsp	canola oil	45 mL
2 Tbsp	balsamic vinegar	30 mL
2 Tbsp	honey	30 mL
2 tsp	Dijon mustard	10 mL
½ tsp	salt	2 mL

Directions:

1. Arrange equal amounts of the spinach, onion and beets on each of 4 salad plates.

2. Whisk the dressing ingredients together in a small bowl and spoon equal amounts of the dressing over each. Sprinkle evenly with the almonds.

 About This Recipe: Tried fresh beets before? They add rich colour (red, golden or striped), a clean, sweet flavour and they're packed with nutrients. Now that's a triple threat!

Per Serving: 212 kcal, 14 g fat, 1 g saturated fat, 21 g carbohydrate, 4 g fibre, 3 g protein.

 Quick Tip: Peel raw beets under cold running water to prevent staining fingertips.

 Chef's Tip: For an entrée, add 1 oz (30 g) crumbled blue cheese and 2 cups (500 mL) cooked diced chicken breast meat to the recipe. (This adds 1 Meat and Alternatives serving and 170 kcal per serving.)

Barbecue Chicken Pita Pizza

Serves 4 - Serving Size: 1 pita pizza

Ingredients:

1 cup	diced cooked chicken	250 mL
½ cup	barbecue sauce	125 mL
4	whole-wheat pita breads (6-inches)	4
⅓ cup	real bacon bits	75 mL
1	small onion, halved and thinly sliced	1
1	small green pepper, julienned	1
¼ cup	chopped green chilies	1 can
½ cup	mushroom stems and pieces, drained	1 can
1 cup	shredded cheddar cheese	250 mL

Directions:

1. In a small bowl, combine chicken and barbecue sauce; spoon over pitas. Top with the bacon, onion, green pepper, chilies, mushroom and cheese.

2. Place on an ungreased baking sheet. Bake at 450°F (230°C) for 8-10 minutes or until heated through.

About This Recipe: Such a simple and tasty barbecue chicken pizza. A 15 minute dinner if you have some leftover chicken!

Per Serving: 407 kcal, 8 g fat, 2 g saturated fat, 58 g carbohydrate, 8 g fibre, 28 g protein.

Healthy Tip: Instead of bacon bits, substitute fresh herbs, garlic or ginger.

Quick Tip: This recipe is great for using up leftover veggies, so experiment with those you have on hand. You can easily substitute fresh mushrooms for canned mushrooms. In addition, using low-fat cheddar cheese saves calories and reduces the saturated fat in the diet.

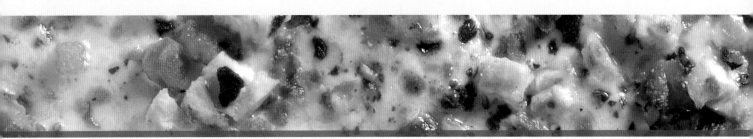

Cookie Crumble Baked Apples

Serves 2 - Serving Size: 1 apple

Ingredients:

2	medium cooking apples (such as McIntosh)	2
2	gingersnap cookies or granola bars, crumbled (see recipes in week 1)	2

Directions:

1. Remove the apple core, cutting from the top of the apple. Don't cut right through to the bottom. Prick the apples with a fork.

2. Fill the core with crumbled cookies or granola bars.

3. Place apples on a dish and microwave them on high for 1 ½ minutes or until apples are tender (or place the apple in a baking pan with 2 Tbsp (30 mL) of water and bake in a 350°F (180°C) oven for 30 minutes.

 About This Recipe: Nothing smells better than baked apples in the evening – or in the morning for breakfast! All they need is a little sprinkle of ginger snap goodness.

Per Serving: 163 kcal, 4 g fat, 0.3 g saturated fat, 34 g carbohydrate, 2 g dietary fibre, 1 g protein.

Canadians eat more apples than any other fruit. Although the prairie provinces aren't known for lush orchards, many varieties are hardy in our climate and can be grown in the backyard. Two apple trees are needed for cross-pollination. Varieties listed as hardy to Zone 3 include Wealthy and Yellow Transparent, both good for baking. The University of Saskatchewan Fruit Program has developed new cultivars that may be available in local tree nurseries.

Head to Head: How the Nutrients Stack Up

Dairy Products: One serving of milk has the highest amount of vitamin A and vitamin D of the dairy options. Cheddar cheese is higher in saturated fat per serving but it's a great source of protein, calcium and vitamin A. In PPEP, we recommend low-fat yogurt over ice cream because it's higher in protein, lower in fat and has twice as much calcium per serving.

	Milk 1% milkfat 250 mL	Yogurt 1% MF, vanilla 175 mL	Cheddar regular 50 g	Ice Cream regular, vanilla 125 mL
Energy (kcal)	108	183	202	153
Protein (g)	9	7	12	3
Carbohydrate (g)	13	30	1	18
Total Fat (g)	3	4	17	8
Saturated fat (g)	1.6	2.3	10.5	5.2
Calcium (mcg)	307	227	361	97
Vitamin A (RAE)	150	n/a	133	90
Vitamin D (mcg)*	2.6	n/a	0.1	n/a

*Many prairie-dwellers have low vitamin D because of the long winters and lack of sunlight exposure. Some brands of yogurt and cheese are made with vitamin D-fortified milk, so check labels.

Week 2, Day 3

Meal	Ingredients per Serving	Canada's Food Guide Servings
Breakfast Scrambled Eggs with Cheese (recipe follows)	1 serving Scrambled Eggs with Cheese 1 slice whole-wheat toast ½ grapefruit 1 cup (250 mL) coffee / tea 2 Tbsp (30 mL) 1% milk (optional) 1 tsp (5 mL) granulated sugar (optional)	1 Vegetables and Fruit 1 Grain Products 1 Meat and Alternatives ½ Milk and Alternatives 1 Oils and Fats
Morning Snack Apple with Peanut Butter	1 apple 1 Tbsp (15 mL) peanut butter	1 Vegetables and Fruit ½ Meat and Alternatives
Lunch Zesty Chicken Wraps (recipe follows)	1 serving Zesty Chicken Wraps ½ cup (125 mL) apple juice	1 ¼ Vegetables and Fruit 2 Grain Products 1 ½ Meat and Alternatives 1 Milk and Alternatives 2 Oils and Fats
Afternoon Snack Whole-wheat Pita with Greek-style Dip (recipe follows)	½ whole-wheat pita 1 serving Greek-style Dip	1 Grain Products ½ Milk and Alternatives
Dinner Vegetarian Chili Chowder (recipe follows)	1 serving Vegetarian Chili Chowder 1 slice rye bread 1 tsp (5 mL) non-hydrogenated margarine	4 Vegetables and Fruit 1 Grain Products 1 Meat and Alternatives 1 Oils and Fats
Evening Snack Strawberry Bran Muffin and Milk (recipe follows)	1 Strawberry Bran Muffin 1 cup (250 mL) 1% milk	1 Grain Products 1 Milk and Alternatives
Total Servings:		7 ¼ Vegetables and Fruit 6 Grain Products 4 Meat and Alternatives 3 Milk and Alternatives 4 Oils and Fats

Good To Know

Nutrition facts of the day	Adjusting today's menu
Calories: 2045 Fat: 74 g Saturated fat: 18 g Carbohydrate: 265 g Fibre: 31 g Protein: 96 g	*To cut about 200 calories* · Have 1 scrambled egg at breakfast, using half the amount of cheese and oil (saves 175 kcal) · Have ⅓ of pita at afternoon snack (saves 25 kcal) *To add about 200 calories* · Add 1 more Tbsp (15 mL) peanut butter (adds 90 kcal) and ¾ cup (175 mL) 1% milk (adds 75 kcal) to morning snack · Add ½ small grapefruit to afternoon snack (adds 40 kcal)

Scrambled Eggs with Cheese

Serves 2 - Serving Size: 2 eggs

Ingredients:

4	large eggs	4
½ cup	shredded low-fat cheese of choice	125 mL
½ tsp	salt and freshly ground black pepper	2 mL
1 Tbsp	milk, cream or water, optional	15 mL
1 Tbsp	butter or canola oil	15 mL

Directions:

1. Beat the eggs lightly with some salt and pepper and the milk, if using.

2. Put the butter or oil in a medium skillet, preferably non-stick, over medium-high heat. When the butter is melted or the canola oil is hot, add the eggs. Cook, stirring frequently and scraping the sides of the pan (A heat proof rubber spatula is a good tool here.)

3. As eggs begin to set, stir in ½ cup (125 mL) grated cheese (use any kind of cheese you like except the ones that don't melt easily, like feta or queso fresco).

4. As the eggs begin to curdle, you may notice that some parts are drying out. Whenever you see that, remove the pan from the heat and continue to stir until the cooking slows down a bit. Then return to the heat and continue cooking.

5. The eggs are done when creamy, soft and still a bit runny; do not overcook unless you intend to. Serve immediately.

 About This Recipe: Sometimes you just need a good solid scrambled egg recipe. Perfect ratio of cheese to egg to awesome.

Per Serving: 351 kcal, 28 g fat, 6 g saturated fat, 1 g carbohydrate, 0 fibre, 23 g protein.

 Quick Tip: While olive oil is known for its health benefits and flavour, canola oil is a good choice since it's heart healthy, local, and less expensive. And, for those who like the flavour of oils, there's cold-press canola oils as well.

Zesty Chicken Wraps
Serves 6 - Serving Size: 1 wrap

Ingredients:

¼ cup	canola oil	60 mL
2 Tbsp	lime juice	30 mL
2	cloves garlic, minced	2
½ tsp	ground cumin	2 mL
2 tsp	ground fennel	10 mL
1 Tbsp	grated lime zest	15 mL
2 tsp	chopped fresh mint	10 mL
2 Tbsp	chopped fresh cilantro	30 mL
4	large skinless, boneless chicken breasts, cut into ½-inch (1 cm) strips	4
6	small tomatoes, seeded and chopped	6
4	green onions, chopped	4
½	English cucumber, diced	½
6	whole-wheat tortilla wraps low or no-fat sour cream	6

Directions:

1. In large bowl, combine canola oil, lime juice, garlic, cumin, fennel, lime zest, mint and cilantro. Add chicken to bowl and toss to coat chicken pieces with mixture. Let stand for 15 minutes.

2. In large non-stick frying pan, cook chicken mixture over medium-high heat for 6-8 minutes or until chicken juices run clear.

3. Place chicken on wrap. Add tomato, green onion, cucumber and a dollop of sour cream. Fold and serve immediately.

About This Recipe: What a fresh way to dress up your chicken. The cumin and fennel add some complexity while the mint and cilantro keep it fresh!

Per Serving: 537 kcal, 21 g fat, 5 g saturated fat, 61 g carbohydrate, 8 g fibre, 30 g protein.

Quick Tip: Turn this wrap into a tasty vegetarian option by substituting your favourite canned bean or diced firm tofu for the chicken.

Greek-Style Dip
Serves 4 - Serving Size: ⅓ cup (100 mL)

Ingredients:

1 cup	low-fat plain yogurt	250 mL
½ cup	grated cucumber, pressed to remove water	125 mL
1 Tbsp	freshly squeezed lemon juice	15 mL
1	clove garlic, minced	1

Directions:

1. In a small bowl, combine yogurt, cucumber, lemon juice, and garlic. Cover and refrigerate until ready to serve.

 About This Recipe: Quality ingredients really make this dish shine. Yes, fresh garlic and fresh lemon juice are necessary. That is how the Greeks do it!

Per Serving: 42 kcal, 1 g fat, 0.6 g saturated fat, 5 g carbohydrate, 0.1 g fibre, 3 g protein.

 Quick Tip: Try serving this excellent sauce with grilled chicken, salmon or lamb. This topping will keep for 2-3 days in the refrigerator.

Consumption of milk by Canadians has been decreasing in recent years. Research conducted at the University of Alberta found that people are eating more yogurt, influenced by the variety of brands, package sizes and uses for yogurt.

Vegetarian Chili Chowder

Serves 4 - Serving Size: Approximately 1 ½ cups (375 mL)

Ingredients:

	canola oil cooking spray	
¼ cup	onion	60 mL
1 Tbsp	jalapeno pepper ribs and seeds removed, chopped	15 mL
¼ cup	celery, chopped	60 mL
1	clove garlic, minced	1
2 tsp	chili powder	10 mL
½ tsp	ground cumin	2 mL
½ tsp	smoked paprika	2 mL
1 tsp	dried mustard	5 mL
1 cup	no-added-salt diced tomatoes, undrained	250 mL
½ cup	no-added-salt tomato sauce	125 mL
1 Tbsp	white wine vinegar	15 mL
1 cup	great northern or pinto beans, drained and rinsed	250 mL
1 cup	potatoes, diced	250 mL
½ cup	corn kernels, fresh, frozen or canned (drained)	125 mL
½ cup	carrots, diced	125 mL
½ cup	low-sodium vegetable broth	125 mL
pinch	chipotle chili pepper	pinch
dash	freshly ground pepper	dash
	Tabasco sauce (optional)	

Directions:

1. Lightly spray non-stick medium saucepan with canola oil spray. Heat saucepan.

2. Cook onion, jalapeno pepper, celery and garlic for about 2-3 minutes or until softened. Add spices; cook, stirring, for 1 minute. Add tomatoes, beans, potatoes, corn and vegetable stock; bring to a boil.

3. Reduce heat and simmer for 15-20 minutes or until potatoes are tender and chowder has thickened. Season with pepper and chipotle chili if desired.

4. For added zing, add 1-2 mL (¼-½ tsp) Tabasco sauce.

 About This Recipe: So full of flavour, filling, and comforting you won't even guess that this chili is vegetarian!
Per Serving: 281 kcal, 2 g fat, 0.2 g saturated fat, 56 g carbohydrate, 7 g fibre, 12 g protein.

Strawberry Bran Muffin

Serves 12 - Serving Size: 1 muffin

Ingredients:

1 ½ cups	natural bran	375 mL
½ cup	whole-wheat flour	125 mL
½ cup	all-purpose flour	125 mL
¼ cup	granulated sugar	60 mL
1 ½ tsp	baking powder	7 mL
½ tsp	baking soda	2 mL
1	large egg, beaten	1
1 cup	low-fat buttermilk	250 mL
2 ½ Tbsp	canola oil	40 mL
¼ cup	molasses	60 mL
½ cup	diced strawberries, fresh or frozen	125 mL

Directions:

1. Preheat oven to 375°F (190°C).

2. In large bowl, mix together bran, flours, sugar, baking powder and baking soda.

3. In another smaller bowl, combine egg, buttermilk, canola oil and molasses; pour into bran mixture and stir just enough to moisten, being careful not to over mix. Fold in strawberries.

4. Divide mixture evenly into non-stick muffin tins. Bake in preheated oven for 15-20 minutes or until a toothpick inserted into the centre comes out clean. Remove from oven and let stand for 2 minutes before removing muffins from tin.

About This Recipe: The buttermilk adds some tang, and provides the muffin with a softer texture without adding much fat!

Per Serving: 134 kcal, 4 g fat, 0.7 g saturated fat, 23 g carbohydrate, 4 g fibre, 4 g protein.

Healthy Tip: Wheat bran is a source of dietary fibre. Canadians should consume 26-35 g of fibre daily. The insoluble fibre of wheat bran also combats constipation.

Quick Tip: If you don't stock buttermilk, make soured milk by adding 1 Tbsp (15 mL) white vinegar to a measuring cup, then adding milk up to 1 cup (250 mL).

Week 2, Day 4

Meal	Ingredients per Serving	Canada's Food Guide Servings
Breakfast Shreddies with Strawberries and Milk	¾ cup (175 mL) Post Shreddies ½ cup (125 mL) strawberries ½ cup (125 mL) 1% milk 1 cup (250 mL) coffee / tea 2 Tbsp (30 mL) 1% milk (optional) 1 tsp (5 mL) granulated sugar (optional)	1 Vegetables and Fruit 1 Grain Products ½ Milk and Alternatives
Morning Snack Yogurt and Granola	¾ cup (175 mL) low-fat yogurt 2 Tbsp (30 mL) low-fat granola	½ Grain Products 1 Milk and Alternatives
Lunch Tuna Salad Pockets with Milk (recipe follows)	1 serving Tuna Salad Pockets 1 cup (250 mL) 1% milk	2 Grain Products 1 ½ Meat and Alternatives 1 Milk and Alternatives
Afternoon Snack Apple and Cheese	1 apple ¾ oz (22 g) low-fat cheddar cheese	1 Vegetables and Fruit ½ Milk and Alternatives
Dinner Orange Chicken and Veggies with Rice and Tossed Salad (recipe follows)	1 serving Orange Chicken and Veggies with Rice 1 cup (250 mL) shredded romaine lettuce ¼ cup (60 mL) each sliced cucumber and carrots 1 Tbsp (15 mL) low-fat balsamic vinaigrette	2 ½ Vegetables and Fruit 1 Grain Products 1 ½ Meat and Alternatives 2 ½ Oils and Fats
Evening Snack Raisin Toast and Orange	1 slice raisin toast with 2 tsp (10 mL) jam 1 mandarin orange 1 cup (250 mL) water	1 Vegetables and Fruit 1 Grain Products
Total Servings:		5 ¾ Vegetables and Fruit 5 ½ Grain Products 3 Meat and Alternatives 3 Milk and Alternatives 2 ½ Oils and Fats

Good To Know

Nutrition facts of the day	Adjusting today's menu
Calories: 1921 Fat: 47 g Saturated fat: 11 g Carbohydrate: 270 g Fibre: 25 g Protein: 116 g	*To cut about 200 calories* · Omit walnuts and pickle relish at lunch (saves 125 kcal) · Reduce rice (uncooked) to ¼ cup (60 mL) per serving at dinner (saves 45 kcal) · Reduce toast to half a serving at evening snack (saves 50 kcal) *To add about 200 calories* · Increase milk to 1 cup (250 mL) at breakfast (adds 50 kcal) · Increase granola to ⅓ cup (75 mL) at morning snack (adds 60 kcal) · Have 1 Tbsp (15 mL) peanut butter with the apple at afternoon snack (adds 90 kcal)

Tuna Salad Pockets

Serves 2 - Serving Size: 2 pita halves with filling

Ingredients:

1 can	6 oz (170 g) tuna, drained and flaked	1 can
¼ cup	thinly sliced celery	60 mL
¼ cup	chopped walnuts	60 mL
¼ cup	plain yogurt	60 mL
3 Tbsp	sweet pickle relish	45 mL
1	green onion, sliced	1
2	6-inch (15 cm) whole-wheat wraps or pita breads, halved	2

Directions:

1. In a small bowl, combine the first six ingredients and mix well.

2. Spoon into whole-wheat wraps or pitas.

About This Recipe: The walnuts really round out the flavour of this tuna salad while providing a boost of heart-healthy omega-3s!

Per Serving: 487 kcal, 19 g fat, 3 g saturated fat, 48 g carbohydrate, 6 g fibre, 35 g protein.

Healthy Tip: Canned salmon works great in this recipe if you want to switch it up. Simply drain well. Select canned salmon with bones, and there's the added bonus of a great, easily absorbed source of calcium.

Orange Chicken and Veggies with Rice

Serves 4 - Serving Size: 4 oz (115 g) chicken breast, ½ cup rice

Ingredients:

1 ½ cups	uncooked rice	375 mL
1 Tbsp	cornstarch	15 mL
1 cup	orange juice	250 mL
1 Tbsp	soy sauce	15 mL
1 tsp	granulated sugar	5 mL
¼ tsp	salt	1 mL
¼ tsp	pepper	1 mL
¼ cup	cornstarch	60 mL
1 lb	boneless chicken	450 g
3 Tbsp	canola oil, divided	45 mL
1 ½ cups	sliced fresh carrots	375 mL
1 cup	chopped green pepper	250 mL
½ cup	chopped onion	125 mL

Directions:

1. Prepare rice according to package directions. Meanwhile, in a small bowl, combine 1 Tbsp (15 mL) cornstarch, orange juice, soy sauce, sugar, salt and pepper; set aside.

2. Place remaining cornstarch ¼ cup (60 mL) in a large resealable plastic bag. Add chicken, a few pieces at a time, and shake to coat. In a large skillet over medium heat, cook chicken in 2 Tbsp (30 mL) oil for 7-9 minutes or until chicken juices run clear. Remove and keep warm.

3. In the same skillet, sauté carrots in remaining oil for 2 minutes. Add green pepper and onion, sauté for 2-3 minutes longer or until vegetables are crisp-tender. Stir cornstarch mixture and add to the pan. Bring to a boil; cook and stir for 2 minutes or until thickened. Add chicken; heat through. Serve with rice.

About This Recipe: Perfect dinner to eat in the sunshine or if you need some more sun in your day!

Per Serving: 554 kcal, 15 g fat, 2 g saturated fat, 63 g carbohydrate, 3 g fibre, 39 g protein.

Healthy Tip: Instant rice has a higher glycemic index that raises your blood sugar faster compared with other grains. You can replace it with healthier alternatives such as basmati rice, brown rice, parboiled rice, barley or even whole-wheat pasta.

Quick Tip: Substitute smashed (potatoes cooked with the peel that are mashed) with low-fat milk or low-sodium chicken broth, if preferred.

Potatoes

Unlike wheat and rice, potatoes are native to the Americas and were first grown in Bolivia and Peru. Early explorers took them to Europe before bringing them to North America.

About half of the vegetables Canadians eat are potatoes. We grow a lot of potatoes, too, in every province. According to the *Canadian Encyclopedia*, the annual Canadian potato crop is worth $1 billion. Manitoba and Alberta rank second and fourth in total potato production.

One medium potato, boiled with the skin on has about 130 kcal, no fat, 30 g carbohydrate, 2.5 g fibre and 3 g protein. When eaten with the skin, one potato can provide nearly half of your vitamin C requirement as well as being a good source of potassium and vitamin B_6. Avoid eating French-fried potatoes or potato chips as they add fats and salt to your diet. Instead, maximize the down-home goodness of potatoes by baking, boiling or roasting them.

Week 2, Day 5

Meal	Ingredients per Serving	Canada's Food Guide Servings
Breakfast Breakfast Zucchini Muffins (recipe follows)	1 Breakfast Zucchini Muffin ½ cup (125 mL) strawberries 1 cup (250 mL) coffee / tea 2 Tbsp (30 mL) 1% milk (optional) 1 tsp (5 mL) granulated sugar (optional)	1 ½ Vegetables and Fruit 1 Grain Products
Morning Snack Bagel with Cheese	½ whole-grain or whole-wheat bagel ¾ oz (22 g) low-fat mozzarella cheese	1 Grain Products ½ Milk and Alternatives
Lunch Minestrone with Mucho Meatballs (recipe follows)	1 serving Minestrone with Mucho Meatballs ½ whole-wheat pita 1 cup (250 mL) 1% milk	3 Vegetables and Fruit 1 ½ Grain Products ½ Meat and Alternatives 1 Milk and Alternatives
Afternoon Snack Cranberry, Egg and Spinach Salad	1 cup (250 mL) spinach 1 hard boiled egg, chopped 2 Tbsp (30 mL) dried cranberries 1 Tbsp (15 mL) low-fat balsamic vinaigrette 1 Tbsp (15 mL) crumbled feta cheese	1 ½ Vegetables and Fruit ½ Meat and Alternatives 1 Oils and Fats
Dinner Fish Tacos with Avocado Salsa and Green Beans with Tomatoes (recipes follow)	1 serving Fish Tacos with Avocado Salsa 1 serving Green Beans with Tomatoes	3 ¼ Vegetables and Fruit 4 Grain Products 2 ½ Meats and Alternatives 3 ½ Oils and Fats
Evening Snack Chocolate Milk Jiggle Pudding (recipe follows)	1 serving Chocolate Milk Jiggle Pudding 2 Tbsp (30 mL) sunflower seeds	½ Meat and Alternatives 1 ½ Milk and Alternatives
Total Servings:		9 ¼ Vegetables and Fruit 7 ½ Grain Products 4 Meat and Alternatives 3 Milk and Alternatives 4 ½ Oils and Fats

Good To Know

Nutrition facts of the day	Adjusting today's menu
Calories: 2212 Fat: 70 g Saturated fat: 17 g Carbohydrate: 288 g Fibre: 33 g Protein: 113 g	*To cut about 200 calories* · Make the Minestrone Soup without meatballs at lunch (saves 100 kcal) · Skip pita bread at lunch (saves 85 kcal) *To add about 200 calories* · Add ½ cup (125 mL) low-fat yogurt to morning snack (adds 80 kcal) · Add 1 Tbsp (15 mL) salsa with 1 Tbsp (15 mL) hummus as a spread for pita bread at lunch (adds 20 kcal) · Mix ¼ cup (60 mL) each chopped medium avocado into the salad at afternoon snack (adds 80 kcal)

Breakfast Zucchini Muffins
Serves 12 - Serving Size: 1 muffin

Ingredients:

	canola oil cooking spray	
1 Tbsp	granulated sugar	15 mL
¼ tsp	ground cinnamon	1 mL
1 ½ cups	quick cooking oats	375 mL
⅔ cup	all-purpose flour	150 mL
½ cup	granulated sugar	125 mL
1 ¼ tsp	ground cinnamon	6 mL
2 tsp	baking powder	10 mL
½ tsp	ground nutmeg	2 mL
¼ tsp	salt	1 mL
¾ cup	1% or skim milk	175 mL
¼ cup	canola oil	60 mL
1	large egg	1
1 ½ tsp	vanilla extract	7 mL
1 Tbsp	grated orange zest or lemon zest	15 mL
1 ½ cups	shredded zucchini	375 mL
2 Tbsp	ground flaxseed	30 mL

Directions:

1. Preheat the oven to 400°F (200°C). Lightly spray a non-stick 12-cup muffin pan with cooking spray.

2. Stir together 1 Tbsp (15 mL) of the sugar and ¼ tsp (1 mL) of the cinnamon in a small bowl and set aside.

3. Stir together the oats, flour, the remaining sugar and cinnamon, baking powder, nutmeg and salt in a large bowl.

4. Whisk together the milk, canola oil, egg, vanilla and grated zest in a medium bowl. Add the zucchini and stir until well blended.

5. Make a well in the flour mixture, add the zucchini mixture and stir until just blended. Spoon the batter into the muffin cups. Sprinkle the flax evenly over all.

6. Bake for 15 minutes, or until toothpick inserted comes out clean. Sprinkle the cinnamon sugar evenly over the muffins.

7. Place muffin tin on wire rack and let stand for 5 minutes before gently removing muffins. Cool completely.

 About This Recipe: The zucchini in this recipe is like a secret weapon. It ensures the muffins keep moist and adds vitamins and minerals.

Per Serving: 177 kcal, 6 g fat, 0.6 g saturated fat, 26 g carbohydrate, 2 g fibre, 4 g protein.

 Quick tip: Even better the next day! These muffins freeze well and are great to have on hand.

Minestrone with Mucho Meatballs

Serves 4 - Serving Size: 2 cups (500 mL)

Ingredients:

½	slice whole-wheat bread, crust removed	½
2 cups	low-sodium chicken broth	500 mL
½ lb	ground beef, lean or extra-lean	225 g
¼ tsp	salt	1 mL
⅛ tsp	ground pepper, divided	0.5 mL
¾ tsp	Italian seasoning, divided	4 mL
2	cloves garlic, minced	2
½	large onion, chopped	½
½	carrot, thinly sliced	½
½	celery stalk, thinly sliced	½
⅛ tsp	chili pepper flakes (optional)	0.5 mL
1 can	14 oz (398 mL) diced tomatoes	1 can
½ can	7.5 oz (213 mL) tomato paste	½ can
1 ½ cups	kale, chopped	375 mL
¼ cup	whole-wheat spaghetti, broken	60 mL

Directions:

Meatballs:

1. Place bread in large bowl. Moisten with ¼ cup (60 mL) of the broth. Let stand for 5 minutes. Using fork, stir to form paste.

2. Add ground beef, salt, pepper, half of the Italian seasoning and half the garlic. Gently work together. Shape into about twelve 1-inch (2.5 cm) balls; cover and refrigerate. Make ahead: cover and refrigerate for 1 hour or up to 1 day.

Soup:

1. Cook onion, remaining garlic, carrot, celery, remaining Italian seasoning, and chili pepper flakes (if using) in Dutch oven, stirring occasionally over medium-high heat until vegetables soften, about 5 minutes.

2. Add tomatoes, remaining chicken broth and tomato sauce; bring to boil. Drop meatballs into sauce; reduce heat, cover and simmer for 15 minutes.

3. Add kale and pasta; simmer for 10 minutes or until pasta is tender.

About This Recipe: A warm and hearty soup that satisfies your taste buds and your daily nutrient requirements! The kale adds loads of vitamin C, vitamin K and minerals.

Per Serving: 356 kcal, 4 g fat, 0.8 g saturated fat, 58 g carbohydrate, 8 g fibre, 22 g protein.

Healthy Tip: Substitute spinach for the kale if desired; but, add spinach only in the last few minutes of cooking so that it wilts, but does not become 'mush'. Both kale and spinach are dark green vegetables - you should try to have at least one serving of dark green vegetables every day (see page 21).

Fish Tacos
with Avocado Salsa

Serves 4 - Serving Size: 4 oz (115 g) cooked fish

Ingredients:

¼ cup	all-purpose flour, spooned into measuring cup and levelled	60 mL
¼ cup	cornmeal	60 mL
½ tsp	onion powder	2 mL
½ tsp	chili powder	2 mL
4	fish fillets 1 lb (450 g) such as tilapia, rinsed, patted dry, and cut into 8 strips	4
2 Tbsp	canola oil	30 mL
¼ tsp	salt	1 mL
8	corn tortillas, warmed	8
½	medium avocado, peeled, pitted and diced	½
½ cup	fresh pico de gallo, salsa verde, or picante sauce	125 mL
1	medium lime, cut into 8 wedges	1

Directions:

1. Combine flour, cornmeal, onion powder, and chili powder in a shallow dish, such as a pie pan. Coat fish with mixture.

2. Heat canola oil in a large non-stick skillet over medium high heat. Add fish; cook for 3 minutes on each side until browned and fish flakes with a fork. Place on a serving platter and sprinkle evenly with salt.

3. Place fish in warmed tortillas, and top with equal amounts of avocado and pico de gallo (or other sauce). Squeeze a lime wedge over each tortilla.

About This Recipe: A creative, healthy twist on the original American taco. Lighter flavours, less fat, more nutrients and a fresher feeling when you're finished!

Per Serving: 439 kcal, 18 g fat, 3 g saturated fat, 45 g carbohydrate, 8 g fibre, 29 g protein.

Quick Tip: Having trouble picking avocado at the grocery store? Choose avocados that have an even, unblemished skin, with a uniform texture throughout, with no soft spots. You will know it's ripe if it yields when you press with your thumb. It is best to select unripe avocados and let them ripen at home on the counter.

Green Beans with Tomatoes

Serves 4 - Serving Size: 1 cup (250 mL)

Ingredients:

1 lb	fresh or frozen cut green beans	450 g
20	cherry tomatoes, quartered	20
½ cup	Italian salad dressing	125 mL

Directions:

1. Place beans in a large saucepan. Add ½ cup (125 mL) water, bring to a boil.

2. Reduce heat and cook, uncovered for 8-10 minutes or until crisp-tender. Drain.

3. Add the tomatoes and salad dressing; toss to coat.

About This Recipe: This recipe allows each ingredient to show you what it's about -- Interesting flavour and great nutrition! For a nice lunch, add 1 cup (250 mL) chick peas.

Per Serving: 128 kcal, 6 g fat, 0.9 g saturated fat, 15 g carbohydrate, 3 g fibre, 2 g protein.

Healthy Tip: Choose a low-fat or low-calorie Italian dressing instead of regular ones. Try adding only half of the dressing and mix in spices and herbs such as black pepper, parsley, basil and thyme to your taste. Alternatively, try cold press canola oil and balsamic vinegar.

Chocolate Milk Jiggle Pudding

Serves 6 - Serving Size: ½ cup (125 mL)

Ingredients:

¼ cup	1% milk	60 mL
3 cups	low-fat chocolate milk, divided	750 mL
1	7 g envelope unflavoured gelatin	1

Directions:

1. Sprinkle gelatin over white milk in small bowl. Let stand for 10 minutes.

2. Meanwhile, heat 1 cup (250 mL) of chocolate milk in a small saucepan over medium heat until steaming; do not boil. Remove from heat.

3. Add gelatin mixture and whisk until dissolved. Whisk in remaining chocolate milk.

4. Divide mixture into 4 individual serving glasses. Refrigerate for about 4 hours or overnight until set.

 About This Recipe: A creative way to snack on some chocolate milk! A low-fat, lower cost alternative to store brought puddings.

Per Serving: 163 kcal, 2 g fat, 1 g saturated fat, 24 g carbohydrate, 13 g protein.

 Quick Tip: Prepare this recipe the night before or early in the day. Top with a dollop of low-fat vanilla yogurt and sprinkle with sunflower seeds if desired.

According to the Dairy Farmers of Canada, chocolate milk contains the same 16 nutrients as white milk, but remember it contains about 13 g of added sugar per cup. If you like chocolate milk for a treat, try a half-and-half mixture with regular milk. That way you'll get all the nutritional benefits and only half the added sugar.

Chocolate milk has been compared with sports drinks by scientists. The evidence suggests that drinking chocolate milk after exercise can enhance exercise recovery of the muscles.

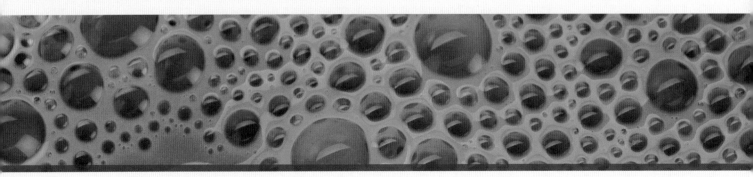

Week 2, Day 6

Meal	Ingredients per Serving	Canada's Food Guide Servings
Breakfast Eggs on English Muffin	2 poached eggs 1 whole-wheat English muffin ½ cup (125 mL) sliced strawberries and kiwifruit 1 cup (250 mL) coffee / tea 2 Tbsp (30 mL) 1% milk (optional) 1 tsp (5 mL) granulated sugar (optional)	1 Vegetables and Fruits 1 ½ Grain Products 1 Meat and Alternatives
Morning Snack Hummus and Pita (see week 1)	1 serving hummus ½ whole-wheat pita	1 Grain Products ½ Meat and Alternatives
Lunch Tomato Soup with Fennel, Leek and Potato with Grilled Cheese Sandwich (recipes follow)	1 serving Tomato Soup with Fennel, Leek and Potato 1 serving Grilled Cheese Sandwich 1 apple	3 ¾ Vegetables and Fruit 2 Grain Products 1 Meat and Alternatives 1 Milk and Alternatives 1 ½ Oils and Fats
Afternoon Snack Veggies with Greek-style Dip (see week 2) and All-Bran Bar	¼ cup (60 ml) sliced zucchini ½ cup (125 mL) snap peas 1 serving Greek-style Dip 1 All-Bran Bar	1 ½ Vegetables and Fruit 1 Grain Products ½ Milk and Alternatives
Dinner Herbed Pork Chops and Roasted Fingerling Potatoes (recipe follows)	1 serving Herbed Pork Chops and Roasted Fingerling Potatoes ½ cup (125 mL) steamed broccoli 1 cup (250 mL) 1% milk	3 ¼ Vegetables and Fruit 1 ½ Meats and Alternatives 1 Milk and Alternatives ½ Oils and Fats
Evening Snack Berry Good For You Cookies and Yogurt (recipe follows)	1 Berry Good For You Cookie ½ cup (125 mL) low-fat yogurt	½ Grain Products ½ Milk and Alternatives
Total Servings:		9 ½ Vegetables and Fruit 6 Grain Products 4 Meat and Alternatives 3 Milk and Alternatives 2 Oils and Fats

Good To Know

Nutrition facts of the day	Adjusting today's menu
Calories: 1737 Fat: 57 g Saturated fat: 14 g Carbohydrate: 233 g Fibre: 32 g Protein: 84 g	*To cut about 200 calories* · Make a lighter grilled cheese sandwich - use only 1 slice ¾ oz (22 g) of cheese and reduce turkey to 1 ¼ oz (38 g) per serving (saves 70 kcal) · Skip All-Bran Bar at afternoon snack (saves 130 kcal) *To add about 200 calories* · Drink 1 cup (250 mL) of 1% milk with your breakfast (adds 100 kcal) · Add ¼ cup (60 mL) cooked black bean (or other types of bean you have) to the pita bread at morning snack (adds 50 kcal) · Increase roasted potatoes to 1 cup (250 mL) per serving at dinner (adds 50 kcal)

Tomato Soup with Fennel, Leek and Potato

Serves 4-6 - Serving Size: 1 cup (250 mL)

Ingredients:

3 Tbsp	canola oil	45 mL
1 tsp	fennel seed, coarsely crushed or ground in a spice grinder	5 mL
1	fennel bulb, trimmed, cored and cut into small dice, about 2 cups (500 mL). Save some fronds for optional garnish	1
1	large leek (white and light-green parts only), halved lengthwise, rinsed well and cut into small dice, about 1 cup (250 mL)	1
1 Tbsp	pernod (optional)	15 mL
3 cups	low-salt chicken broth	750 mL
1 can	16 oz (450 mL) whole peeled plum tomatoes, drained and coarsely chopped (reserve the juice)	1 can
1	medium red or yellow potato, peeled and cut into medium dice	1
	salt and freshly ground black pepper	

Directions:

1. In a non-reactive 4-quart saucepan, heat the oil over medium-low heat. Add the fennel seed and cook until fragrant and lightly brown, about 3 minutes. Add the fennel bulb, leek, and Pernod (if using) and cook over low heat, stirring occasionally, until the vegetables are soft, about 10 minutes.

2. Add the broth, tomatoes, and potato. Bring to a boil over medium heat. Reduce the heat to low, cover, and simmer until the potatoes are cooked through, 30-40 minutes. Season to taste with salt and pepper. Serve chunky or purée in a blender. If you purée the soup and it is too thick, add some of the reserved tomato juice.

3. Serve immediately. Garnish with chopped fennel fronds, or parsley, if desired.

 About This Recipe: The fennel adds a unique flavour twist to a classic tomato soup. The leek adds texture and vitamins K and A!

Per Serving: 124 kcal, 7 g fat, 0.5 g saturated fat, 13 g carbohydrate, 3 g fibre, 3 g protein.

Grilled Cheese Sandwich
Serves 2 - Serving Size: 1 sandwich

Ingredients:

4 slices	low-fat cheese of choice swiss, mozzarella, cheddar, etc. (3 oz in total)	85 g
4 slices	whole-wheat bread	4 slices
5 oz	sliced cooked turkey	140 g
4 slices	tomato	4 slices
4 tsp	non-hydrogenated margarine, optional	20 mL

Directions:

1. Place slices of cheese on the bread. Top with turkey, tomato and another slice of bread. Spread 1 tsp (5 mL) margarine on each side of the sandwich if desired.

2. Cook both sides on a skillet until cheese is melted and bread is browned. Serve immediately.

About This Recipe: Such a classic. Who can resist the melted cheese between two slices of perfectly crisped bread?
Per Serving: 365 kcal, 15 g fat, 3 g saturated fat, 31 g carbohydrate, 4 g fibre, 27 g protein.

Healthy Tip: Use sliced, cooked turkey rather than deli meat in this recipe to decrease sodiums.

Herbed Pork Chops
and Roasted Fingerling Potatoes
Serves 4 - Serving Size: 3 oz (85g) cooked pork

Ingredients:

1 lb	fingerling potatoes, halved lengthwise	450 g
1	medium onion, cut in 8 wedges and layers separated	1
1 Tbsp	canola oil	15 mL
1 tsp	chopped fresh rosemary leaves or ½ tsp (2 mL) dried rosemary leaves	5 mL
1 Tbsp	chopped fresh oregano or 1 tsp (5 mL) dried oregano	15 mL
½ tsp	paprika	2 mL
½ tsp	garlic powder	2 mL
4	5oz (40 g) bone-in pork chops	4
½ tsp	salt	2 mL
¼ tsp	black pepper	1 mL

Directions:

1. Place a foil-lined baking sheet in the oven and preheat oven to 500°F (260°C).

2. Combine the potatoes, onions, oil and rosemary in a medium bowl and toss until well coated. Place in a single layer on the baking sheet, reduce the heat to 425°F (220°C) and cook for 10 minutes.

3. Meanwhile, in a small bowl, combine the oregano, paprika and garlic powder. Sprinkle both sides of the pork with the oregano mixture.

4. Push the vegetables to one side of the baking sheet and arrange the pork chops in a single layer on the baking sheet. Bake for 12 minutes or until pork is slightly pink in center. Sprinkle the salt and pepper evenly over all. Let stand for 3 minutes to develop flavours.

 About This Recipe: This combination of herbs pairs perfectly with the pork without overpowering the flavour of the meat. Serve with your choice of vegetables, such as steamed broccoli or a medley of peas, carrots and corn.

Per Serving: 303 kcal, 13 g fat, 2 g saturated fat, 25 g carbohydrate, 2 g fibre, 22 g protein.

 Chef's Tip: For a quick dipping sauce, stir together 3 Tbsp (45 mL) light canola mayonnaise, 1 Tbsp (15 mL) Dijon mustard, 1 Tbsp (15 mL) water and ½ tsp (2 mL) chopped fresh or ¼ tsp (1 mL) dried rosemary. Makes ¼ cup (60 mL) total. Use 1 Tbsp (15 mL) per serving.

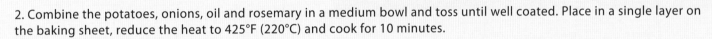

Berry Good For You Cookies

Serves 36 - Serving Size: 1 cookie

Ingredients:

¾ cup	canola oil	175 mL
3	large eggs	3
½ cup	granulated sugar	125 mL
½ cup	brown sugar	125 mL
1 Tbsp	vanilla extract	15 mL
1 ½ cups	whole-wheat flour	375 mL
1 tsp	baking soda	5 mL
¼ tsp	salt	1 mL
1 ½ cups	rolled oats	375 mL
½ cup	flaked coconut	125 mL
1 cup	dried cherries	250 mL
½ cup	dried cranberries	125 mL
½ cup	slivered almonds	125 mL
½ cup	mini chocolate chips	125 mL

Directions:

1. Preheat oven to 350°F (180°C). In large mixing bowl, combine canola oil, eggs, granulated sugar, brown sugar and vanilla. Beat ingredients until well mixed.

2. In small bowl, combine flour, baking soda and salt. Add to canola mixture and stir until just combined.

3. Stir in rolled oats, coconut, cherries, cranberries, almonds and chocolate chips. Mix well.

4. Form dough into 1-inch (2.5 cm) balls and place about 2-inches (5 cm) apart on non-stick cookie sheet lined with parchment paper. Flatten slightly with fork. Bake for 10-12 minutes or until golden brown. Cool for 2 minutes on baking sheet and then remove to wire rack to cool completely.

5. Cool for 2 minutes on baking sheet and remove to wire rack to cool completely.

 About This Recipe: This cookie has got flavour and nutrients. The canola oil and nuts provide healthy fats while the dried fruits add fibre!

Per Serving: 154 kcal, 7 g fat, 1 g saturated fat, 22 g carbohydrate, 2 g fibre, 2 g protein.

 Healthy Tip: Reduce the sugar content of this recipe by using only ⅔ cup (150 mL) of granulated sugar or by using unsweetened coconut.

 Quick Tip: Try something new! Dried cranberries and cherries often come in a variety of flavours.

The Glycemic Index

The Glycemic Index (GI) is a way of rating carbohydrate-rich foods according to how much they raise blood sugar compared with a reference food. White bread or glucose (a pure sugar) is used as a reference food. The maximum score is 100. The Canadian Diabetes Association recommends that people with diabetes think about the GI in meal planning because foods with a low GI can help them control their blood sugars.

Research shows that foods with a low GI are more slowly digested and absorbed from the gut, which means blood sugars will rise more slowly and peak at a lower level than after eating foods with a high GI. The benefit of eating such foods includes lower blood sugars and a healthy balance of blood fats. Eating low GI foods makes people feel full longer, helping with weight control.

The GI concept was developed by researchers at the University of Toronto in the 1980s. Since then, studies have shown that consuming low GI diets is associated with lower risk of developing diabetes and cardiovascular disease. Additional studies have shown that, for people with type 1 or type 2 diabetes, replacing high GI foods with lower GI foods can help improve blood sugar control and reduce episodes of low blood sugar in people taking insulin.

In PPEP, low to medium GI foods are incorporated into the menus and recipes by favouring whole grains including beans, chickpeas, lentils, barley and brown rice. We recommend eating whole fruits with the skin on where practical while limiting fruit juice to one serving per day or less. We also take into account proper serving sizes since the total effect of a food on blood sugar depends on the amount eaten.

Cooking methods also affect GI. For example, boiling potatoes, letting them cool and then reheating them lowers their GI. Cooking pasta to *al dente* (firm, slightly chewy) results in lower GI. Finally, eating high carbohydrate foods within a meal containing protein and fat will slow absorption of the sugars and result in overall lower increases in blood sugars. In PPEP, we often pair carbohydrate-containing snacks with a glass of milk to create this effect.

Week 2, Day 7

Meal	Ingredients per Serving	Canada's Food Guide Servings
Breakfast Breakfast Banana Split (recipe follows)	1 serving Breakfast Banana Split 1 cup (250 mL) coffee / tea 2 Tbsp (30 mL) 1% milk (optional) 1 tsp (5 mL) granulated sugar (optional)	1 ¼ Vegetables and Fruit ¼ Grain Products ¾ Milk and Alternatives
Morning Snack Breakfast Zucchini Muffin and Banana (see week 2, day 5)	½ Breakfast Zucchini Muffin 1 banana	1 ½ Vegetables and Fruit ½ Grain Products
Lunch Smashed Bean and Veggie Wraps (recipe follows)	1 serving Smashed Bean and Veggie Wraps ½ (125 mL) cup carrot sticks 1 cup (250 mL) 1% milk	2 Vegetables and Fruit 1 Grain Products 1 Meat and Alternatives 1 ½ Milk and Alternatives 1 ½ Oils and Fats
Afternoon Snack Crackers and Cheese	3 large Stone Ground Wheat Thins ¾ oz (22 g) low-fat mozzarella cheese	2 Grain Products ½ Milk and Alternatives
Dinner Best Spaghetti and Meatballs with Salad (recipes follow)	1 serving Best Spaghetti and Meatballs 1 cup (250 mL) chopped romaine lettuce ⅓ cup (75 mL) sliced cucumber 1 Tbsp (15 mL) low-fat balsamic vinaigrette	2 Vegetables and Fruit 1 ½ Grain Products 1 ½ Meat and Alternatives 2 Oils and Fats
Evening Snack Chilled Chai Latte (recipe follows)	1 serving Chilled Chai Latte	1 Milk and Alternatives
Total Servings:		8 Vegetables and Fruit 5 ¼ Grain Products 2 ½ Meat and Alternatives 3 ¾ Milk and Alternatives 3 ½ Oils and Fats

Good To Know

Nutrition facts of the day	Adjusting today's menu
Calories: 1705 Fat: 44 g Saturated fat: 14 g Carbohydrate: 257 g Fibre: 33 g Protein: 87 g	*To cut about 200 calories* · Reduce milk to ½ cup (125 mL) at lunch (saves 50 kcal) · Have only 1 cracker at afternoon snack (saves 60 kcal) · At dinner, reduce spaghetti (cooked) to ½ cup (125 mL) and have 1 meatball instead of 2 (85 g) per serving (saves 90 kcal) *To add about 200 calories* · Increase yogurt to ¾ cup (175 mL) per serving at breakfast (adds 40 kcal) · Have 1 Tbsp (15 mL) peanut butter with the banana at morning snack (adds 90 kcal) · Drink ½ cup (125 mL) apple juice with afternoon snack (adds 60 kcal)

Breakfast Banana Splits

Serves 2 - Serving Size: About 1 ½ cups (375 mL)

Ingredients:

1	medium, firm banana	1
⅓ cup	each blueberries, halved seedless grapes, sliced kiwi and strawberries	100 mL
1 cup	vanilla yogurt	250 mL
½ cup	granola cereal with almonds	125 mL
2	maraschino or fresh cherries with stems	2

Directions:

1. Slice banana in half lengthwise; cut each in half width-wise. Place two pieces of banana in two individual bowls.

2. Top each with ⅔ cup (150 mL) mixed fruit, ½ cup (125 mL) yogurt, ¼ cup (60 mL) granola and 1 cherry.

 About This Recipe: Enjoy this guilt-free banana split for a healthy spin on a classic dessert!

Per Serving: 294 kcal, 3 g fat, 1 g saturated fat, 63 g carbohydrate, 6 g fibre, 9 g protein.

 Healthy Tip: Use low-fat yogurt (1% M.F.) and low-fat granola (2-3 g fat per serving). Use any fresh or frozen fruits you have on hand. Frozen fruit has similar nutrient content as fresh, but can often be more economical, and available when needed.

Smashed Bean and Veggie Pitas

Serves 4 - Serving Size: 1 pita half

Ingredients:

½ can	19 oz (540mL) cannellini or other white beans, rinsed dained and roughly mashed	½ can
¼ cup	fresh basil leaves, chopped	60 mL
1 ½ Tbsp	fresh lemon juice	25 mL
2 Tbsp	canola oil	30 mL
1	medium garlic clove, minced	1
⅛ tsp	salt	0.5 mL
2	whole grain pita rounds, cut in half	2
2 cups	chopped romaine lettuce	500 mL
½ cup	light feta cheese, crumbled	125 mL
½	medium cucumber, diced	½
4	small radishes, thinly sliced	4

Directions:

1. Combine the mashed beans, basil, lemon juice, oil, garlic and salt in a small bowl.

2. Place equal amounts of the lettuce in each of the pita halves. Top with equal amounts of the bean mixture, feta, cucumber and radishes.

About This Recipe: The popular Italian cannellini bean has a mild nutty flavour that packs great nutrition-high protein, low fat with fibre, B vitamins and minerals!

Per Serving: 311 kcal, 12 g fat, 3 g saturated fat, 40 g carbohydrate, 9 g fibre, 14 g protein.

Quick Tip: To mash the beans easily and quickly, place the beans on a flat surface, such as a plastic cutting board or dinner plate and use a fork to mash the beans.

Chef's Tip: Add a spoonful of spicy salsa if you like things hot!

Best Spaghetti and Meatballs

Serves 4 - Serving Size: 1 cup (250 mL) spaghetti, 2 meatballs

Ingredients:

Spaghetti Sauce:

6 Tbsp	chopped onion	90 mL
1 ½ tsp	canola oil	7 mL
1	garlic clove, minced	1
¾ cup	water	175 mL
½ can	14 oz (398 mL) tomato sauce	½ can
1 can	5.5 oz (156 mL) tomato paste	1 can
2 Tbsp	minced fresh parsley	30 mL
¾ tsp	dried basil	4 mL
¾ tsp	salt	4 mL
⅛ tsp	pepper	0.5 mL

Meatballs:

1	large egg, lightly beaten	1
½ cup	soft bread cubes ¼-inch (0.5 cm) pieces	125 mL
6 Tbsp	1% milk	90 mL
¼ cup	Parmesan cheese, grated	60 mL
1	garlic clove, minced	1
¾ tsp	salt	4 mL
⅛ tsp	pepper	0.5 mL
¾ lb	ground beef	340 g
1 ½ tsp	canola oil	7 mL
2 cups	cooked whole-wheat spaghetti	500 mL

Directions:

1. In a Dutch oven over medium heat, sauté onion in canola oil. Add garlic; cook for 1 minute longer. Add the water, tomato sauce and paste, parsley, basil, salt and pepper; bring to a boil. Reduce heat; cover and simmer for 50 minutes.

2. In a large bowl, combine the first seven meatball ingredients. Crumble beef over mixture and mix well. Shape into 1 ½-inch (3 cm) balls.

3. In a large skillet over medium heat, brown meatballs in canola oil until no longer pink; drain. Add to sauce; bring to a boil. Reduce heat; cover and simmer for 1 hour or until flavours are blended, stirring occasionally.

4. Serve with whole-wheat spaghetti.

About This Recipe: Home-made meatballs make this spaghetti recipe stand out from the rest! Treat yourself to a childhood favourite.

Per Serving: 457 kcal, 12 g fat, 3 g saturated fat, 62 g carbohydrate, 11 g fibre, 33 g protein.

Healthy Tip: Ground beef makes this recipe an excellent source of vitamin B_{12} and iron. Make sure to choose extra lean ground beef when you shop to reduce saturated fat in your diet. Add any leftover fresh or frozen veggies to the spaghetti sauce to give this meal a boost in vitamins and fibre.

Chilled Chai Latte
Serves 4 - Serving size: 1 cup (250 mL)

Ingredients:

4 cups	1% milk	1 L
3	chai tea bags	3
1	cinnamon stick	1
1 Tbsp	liquid honey or sugar	15 mL
½ tsp	pure vanilla extract	2 mL
	ice cubes	
	ground cinnamon, for garnish	

Directions:

1. In a medium heavy-bottom saucepan, combine milk, tea bags and cinnamon stick. Heat over medium heat for 12 minutes or until steaming, stirring occasionally. Remove saucepan from heat. Discard tea bags and cinnamon; stir in honey (or sugar) and vanilla. Cool to room temperature then chill completely, at least 3 hours.

2. To serve, pour 1 cup (250 mL) of the milk mixture into each of 4 tall, 16 oz (500 mL) serving glasses. Froth using a milk frother and top glass with ice. Garnish with a pinch of cinnamon and serve with a straw.

Healthy Tip: Try decaffeinated chai to avoid losing sleep. Too little sleep has been associated with increased risk of developing high blood pressure and obesity.

The prairie provinces produce 80% of the Canadian honey crop. Bees are an important pollinator of canola and other crops. The flavour and colour of the honey is influenced by the type of plants they pollinate.

Sources of Week 2 Recipes - From the PANDA Nutrition Team

Nuts, Seeds and Crunch Mix *(developed by Nancy Hughes)*
Greens and Beet Salad with Honey Balsamic Dressing *(developed by Nancy Hughes)*
Cookie Crumble Baked Apples
Greek-style Dip
Breakfast Zucchini Muffins *(developed by Nancy Hughes)*
Grilled Cheese Sandwich
Herbed Pork Chops and Roasted Fingerling Potatoes *(developed by Nancy Hughes)*
Smashed Bean and Veggie Pitas *(developed by Nancy Hughes)*

Used with Permission

Alberta Pulse Growers: Baked Biscuits, Black Bean Burgers, Vegetarian Chili Chowder
CanolaInfo.org: Sweet Potato Fries with Cajun Dipping Sauce, Zesty Chicken Wraps, Berry Good For You Cookies, Fish Tacos with Avocado Salsa, Strawberry Bran Muffin
Alberta Milk: Roasted Butternut Squash Soup, Chocolate Milk Jiggle Pudding
Canada Beef: Minestrone with Mucho Meatballs, Dijon Beef and Greens
Taste of Home: Breakfast Banana Splits, Green Beans with Tomatoes, Best Spaghetti and Meatballs, Barbecue Chicken Pita Pizza, Tuna Salad Pockets, Orange Chicken and Veggies with Rice
The Taunton Press, Inc., Fine Cooking Magazine Feb / March 2008: Tomato Soup with Fennel, Leek and Potato
Dairy Farmers of Canada (chef Anna Olson): Chilled Chai Latte
John Wiley and Sons: Scrambled Eggs with Cheese

For more recipes visit: www.pureprairie.ca

Average Intakes of Week 2:

By Food Group:	By Nutrient Profile:
8 Vegetables and Fruits servings 6 Grains servings 3 Meat and Alternatives servings 3 Milk and Alternatives servings	Total Energy: 1948 kcal 58 g fat (27% of total energy) 14 g saturated fat (7% of total energy) 271 g carbohydrate (56% of total energy) 33 g fibre 99 g protein (20% total energy)

Grocery List Week 3

Food Group	Food Item	
Vegetables & Fruit	Apples*†	Peas, baby, frozen*
	Arugula	Peas, snap, fresh*†
	Bananas†	Pears
	Basil, fresh*†	Peppers, chili / jalapeno†
	Bean sprouts	Peppers*, sweet, green / red / yellow†
	Beets*, fresh or canned†	Potatoes*†
	Blueberries or Saskatoons*, fresh / frozen†	Rhubarb, fresh or frozen*†
	Berries, mixed, fresh or frozen	Romaine lettuce / Salad greens*†
	Broccoli*	Spinach*†
	Cabbage, green*	Strawberries*, fresh or frozen†
	Carrots*†	Tomatoes*, Roma / grape†
	Celery*	Turnip*
	Cilantro*†	Zucchini*†
	Cucumber*†	
	Dill, fresh*	
	Garlic*†	
	Gingerroot	
	Green onion*†	
	Lemons†	
	Limes†	
	Mint, fresh*†	
	Mushrooms*†	
	Onions*, yellow / red / sweet†	
	Oranges†	
	Parsley, fresh*†	
	Parsnip*†	
Grain Products	Baguette or buns, whole grain	
	Bagel, whole-wheat*†	
	Bread, whole-wheat*†	
	Bread, cinnamon raisin	
	English muffin, whole-wheat*†	
	Pita bread, whole-wheat*†	
	Tortillas, whole-wheat / corn†	
Milk & Alternatives	Cheddar cheese, low-fat*	
	Feta cheese*	
	Milk, 1% M.F. or skim*†	
	Mozzarella cheese, low-fat*†	
	Yogurt, low-fat, plain†	
	Yogurt, low-fat, vanilla / fruit*†	
Meat & Alternatives	Chicken breast, boneless, skinless*†	
	Eggs*	
	Ground beef, lean*	
	Hummus (or use recipe provided in week 1)	
	Salmon fillets	
	Sirloin beef steak*†	
	Tenderloin beef steak*	

Prairie-produced foods.
† *Foods also listed in week 2*

Week 3, Day 1

Meal	Ingredients per Serving	Canada's Food Guide Servings
Breakfast Bran Flakes with Blueberries	¾ cup (175 mL) bran flakes ½ cup (125 mL) blueberries ½ cup (125 mL) 1% milk 1 cup (250 mL) coffee / tea 2 Tbsp (30 mL) 1% milk (optional) 1 tsp (5 mL) granulated sugar (optional)	1 Vegetables and Fruit 1 Grain Products ½ Milk and Alternatives
Morning Snack English Muffin and Milk	1 whole-wheat English muffin 1 tsp (5 mL) low-sugar strawberry jam 1 tsp (5 mL) reduced non-hydrogenated margarine ½ cup (125 mL) 1% milk	1 Grain Products ½ Milk and Alternatives 1 Oils and Fats
Lunch Marinated Steak with Melted Onions and Crispy Pear and Cabbage Salad (recipes follow)	1 serving Marinated Steak with Melted Onions 1 serving Crispy Pear and Cabbage Salad ½ cup (125 mL) 1% milk	2 Vegetables and Fruit 2 Grain Products 1 ½ Meat and Alternatives ½ Milk and Alternatives 2 Oils and Fats
Afternoon Snack Celery Sticks and Peanut Butter	½ cup (125 mL) celery sticks 2 Tbsp (30 mL) peanut butter	1 Vegetables and Fruit 1 Meat and Alternatives
Dinner Mixed Grain and Lentil Pilaf (recipe follows)	1 serving Mixed Grain and Lentil Pilaf 1 cup (250 mL) mixed greens or spinach 1 Tbsp (15 mL) salad dressing of choice	3 Vegetables and Fruit 1 Grain Products 1 Meat and Alternatives ½ Milk and Alternatives 1 Oils and Fats
Evening Snack Coconutty Rhubarb Crisp with Yogurt (recipe follows)	1 serving Coconutty Rhubarb Crisp ½ cup (125 mL) low-fat vanilla yogurt	1 ½ Vegetables and Fruit ½ Grain Products ½ Milk and Alternatives
Total Servings:		8 ½ Vegetables and Fruit 5 ½ Grain Products 3 ½ Meat and Alternatives 2 ½ Milk and Alternatives 4 Oils and Fats

Good To Know

Nutrition facts of the day	Adjusting today's menu
Calories: 1938 Fat: 72 g Saturated fat: 17 g Carbohydrate: 248 g Fibre: 33 g Protein: 96 g	*To cut about 200 calories* · Have half English muffin instead of one at morning snack (saves 100 kcal) · Cut the serving size of evening snack in half - reduce it to ½ cup (125 mL) rhubarb crisp with ¼ cup (60 mL) yogurt (saves 140 kcal) *To add about 200 calories* · Add 2 Tbsp (30 mL) sliced almonds to the cereal at breakfast and increase milk to 1 cup (250 mL) (adds 95 kcal) · Add 1 banana to afternoon snack (adds 100 kcal)

Marinated Steak with Melted Onions

Serves 4 - Serving Size: 1 baguette with 4 oz (115 g) steak

Ingredients:

2 Tbsp	barbecue sauce	30 mL
2 Tbsp	salad dressing, Greek or Italian style	30 mL
1 lb	1-inch (2.5 cm) thick top sirloin or inside round marinating steak	450 g
4	cloves garlic, minced pepper and salt	4
2 Tbsp	salad dressing, Greek or Italian style	30 mL
1	sweet onion, sliced	1
4	whole-wheat baguettes or buns, sliced	4
	fresh herbs (to garnish)	

Directions:

1. Combine barbecue sauce, 2 Tbsp (30 mL) of the salad dressing and garlic in sealable freezer bag.

2. Pierce steak all over with fork; add to bag. Refrigerate for 8-12 hours.

3. Take the steak out of the bag and pat dry with paper towel; season with pepper and salt. Discard marinade.

4. Grill over medium-high heat for 3-4 minutes per side for medium-rare. Let rest for 10 minutes.

5. Meanwhile, pan-fry onion in remaining 2 Tbsp (30 mL) salad dressing over medium heat, stirring often until soft and golden, about 10 minutes.

6. To serve, place steak on baguette, add onions. Garnish with fresh herbs.

 About This Recipe: Who said steak was only for dinner? The Greek or Italian salad dressing adds a splash of flavour to this healthy steak sandwich.

Per Serving: 425 kcal, 15 g fat, 4 g saturated fat, 37 g carbohydrate, 2 g fibre, 37 g protein.

 Healthy Tip: Use whole grain baguette or buns for this recipe, and any leafy vegetable for topping, such as romaine, mixed salad greens or spinach.

Crispy Pear and Cabbage Shredded Salad

Serves 4 - Serving Size: Approximately 1 cup (250 mL)

Ingredients:

2 cups	shredded green cabbage	500 mL
¾ cup	shredded carrots	175 mL
1	firm small green pear, thinly sliced and cut into matchstick size pieces	1
½	medium jalapeno, seeded and finely chopped	½
¼ cup	dried cranberries or cherries	60 mL
1 ½ Tbsp	granulated sugar	25 mL
¼ cup	fresh lemon juice	30 mL
1 Tbsp	canola oil	15 mL
1 ½ tsp	grated gingerroot	7 mL
⅛ tsp	salt	0.5 mL

Directions:

1. Combine the cabbage, carrots, pear, jalapeno and dried cranberries or cherries in a large bowl.

2. Stir together the remaining ingredients in a small bowl. Pour over the pear mixture and toss until well mixed.

3. Let stand for 10 minutes to allow flavours to blend.

About This Recipe: This winter-inspired salad is mildly spicy with a kick of ginger.

Per Serving: 118 kcal, 4 g fat, 0.3 g saturated fat, 22 g carbohydrate, 3 g fibre, 1 g protein.

Quick Tip: You may substitute jalapeno with 2 Tbsp (30 mL) finely chopped red bell pepper and ⅛ tsp (0.5 mL) dried pepper flakes. To keep gingerroot fresh longer, peel, cut in chunks and store in the freezer. To use, thaw briefly before grating.

Chef's Tip: Be sure to purchase a firm pear rather than a soft ripe pear for a crunchy, crisp texture and distinctive flavour.

Mixed Grain and Lentil Pilaf

Serves 8 - Serving Size: 1 cup (250 mL)

Ingredients:

4 cups	water	1 L
½ cup	dried lentils, sorted and rinsed	125 mL
¼ cup	uncooked bulgur	60 mL
¼ cup	uncooked quinoa	60 mL
1 Tbsp	canola oil	15 mL
1 cup	diced onions	250 mL
1 cup	diced green or red bell peppers	250 mL
4 oz	sliced mushrooms	115 g
¼ cup	sliced almonds or pecans, toasted	60 mL
¼ cup	chopped Italian parsley or mint	60 mL
1 Tbsp	canola oil	15 mL
½ tsp	salt	2 mL
3 oz	reduced fat feta cheese, crumbled	85 g

Directions:

1. In a large saucepan, bring the water and lentils to a boil over high heat. Reduce the heat to medium-low, cover and cook for 15 minutes.

2. Stir in the bulgur and quinoa. Cover and cook for 10 minutes, or until the lentils are just tender. Drain in a fine mesh sieve.

3. Meanwhile, heat 1 Tbsp (15 mL) of the canola oil in a large skillet over medium high heat. Cook the onions and peppers 4 minutes or until edges begin to brown. Add the mushrooms and cook for 5 minutes or until their edges begin to brown, stirring occasionally.

4. Remove from heat, gently stir in the drained lentil mixture, almonds, parsley, salt and second 1 Tbsp (15 mL) canola oil.

5. Sprinkle with feta cheese and gently fold in until just combined.

 About This Recipe: Need a healthy filling dinner in a hurry? 30 minutes for a rich flavour packed with protein and vitamins!

Per Serving: 370 kcal, 9 g fat, 2 g saturated fat, 39 g carbohydrate, 10 g fibre, 36 g protein.

 Cook Once, Eat Twice or More: This recipe makes an excellent side dish for any kind of meat or poultry with a serving size of ½ cup (125 mL). Refrigerate leftovers and store in an airtight container for maximum freshness.

Coconutty Rhubarb Crisp

Serves 8 - Serving Size: Approximately 1 cup (250 mL)

Ingredients:

6 cups	sliced rhubarb	1.5 L
½ cup	orange or apple juice	125 mL
½ cup	granulated sugar	125 mL
1 Tbsp	non-hydrogenated margarine	15 mL
¼ cup	brown sugar	60 mL
1 tsp	cinnamon	5 mL
¼ cup	whole-wheat flour	60 mL
½ cup	oatmeal	125 mL
2 Tbsp	non-hydrogenated margarine	30 mL
¼ cup	unsweetened coconut	60 mL
¼ cup	coarsely chopped pecans	60 mL

Directions:

1. Preheat oven to 350°F (180°C).

2. Combine rhubarb, juice and granulated sugar in a glass cooking dish. Dot with 1 Tbsp (15 mL) margarine.

3. Combine brown sugar, cinnamon, flour and oatmeal. Blend in 2 Tbsp (30 mL) margarine with fork or a pastry blender until crumbly. Mix in coconut and nuts. Spoon over the rhubarb.

4. Bake for 40 minutes or until fruit bubbles through topping.

 About This Recipe: This dessert will satisfy your sweet tooth and boost your nutrition with whole-wheat flour and oatmeal.

Per Serving: 224 kcal, 9 g fat, 3 g saturated fat, 34 g carbohydrate, 4 g fibre, 3 g protein.

 Chef's Tip: If rhubarb is not available, substitute apples, peaches, pears or berries and reduce the amount of granulated sugar. Use walnuts or almonds if you don't have pecans on hand.

Week 3, Day 2

Meal	Ingredients per Serving	Canada's Food Guide Servings
Breakfast Poached Egg with Toast	1 poached egg 2 slices whole-wheat toast 1 ½ tsp (7.5 mL) ketchup ½ cup (125 mL) canned peaches 1 cup (250 mL) coffee / tea 2 Tbsp (30 mL) 1% milk (optional) 1 tsp (5 mL) granulated sugar (optional)	1 Vegetables and Fruit 2 Grain Products ½ Meat and Alternatives
Morning Snack Blueberry Smoothie	½ cup (125 mL) frozen blueberries 2 Tbsp (30 mL) low-fat plain yogurt ½ cup (125 mL) 1% milk	1 Vegetables and Fruit ¾ Milk and Alternatives
Lunch Mediterranean Chicken Stir-Fry (recipe follows)	1 serving Mediterranean Chicken Stir-Fry ½ cup (125 mL) 1% milk	1 ½ Vegetables and Fruit 1 Grain Products 1 ½ Meat and Alternatives ½ Milk and Alternatives 1 Oils and Fats
Afternoon Snack Bagel and Apple Juice	1 cinnamon raisin bagel 2 tsp (10 mL) non-hydrogenated margarine ½ cup (125 mL) apple juice	1 Vegetables and Fruit 2 Grain Products 2 Oils and Fats
Dinner Orange-Glazed Salmon over Sautéed Spinach (recipe follows)	1 serving Orange-Glazed Salmon over Sautéed Spinach ¾ cup (175 mL) cooked wild rice 1 cup (250 mL) 1% milk	2 Vegetables and Fruit 1 Grain Products 1 Meat and Alternatives 1 Milk and Alternatives 2 Oils and Fats
Evening Snack Roasted Veggie, Fresh Veggie Salsa (recipe follows)	1 serving Roasted Veggie, Fresh Veggie Salsa 6 Melba toast	1 Vegetables and Fruit 1 Grain Product
Total Servings:		7 Vegetables and Fruit 7 Grain Products 3 Meat and Alternatives 2 ¼ Milk and Alternatives 5 Oils and Fats

Good To Know

Nutrition facts of the day	Adjusting today's menu
Calories: 1764 Fat: 50 g Saturated fat: 11 g Carbohydrate: 234 g Fibre: 25 g Protein: 102 g	*To cut about 200 calories* · Have only 1 slice of toast at breakfast (saves 70 kcal) · Have only ½ bagel at afternoon snack (saves 135 kcal) *To add about 200 calories* · Add 1 slice whole-wheat toast to morning snack (adds 70 kcal) · Sprinkle 1 Tbsp (30 mL) crumbled feta cheese over the stir-fry at lunch (adds 25 kcal) · Have 1 Tbsp (30 mL) almond or peanut butter with evening snack (adds 100 kcal)

Mediterranean Chicken Stir-Fry

Serves 4 - Serving Size: 1 ½ cups (375 mL)

Ingredients:

1 ¼ cup	water	310 mL
1 cup	quick-cooking barley	250 mL
1 lb	boneless skinless chicken breasts, cubed	450 g
2 tsp	canola oil	10 mL
1	medium onion, chopped	1
2	medium zucchini, chopped	2
1 tsp	canola oil	5 mL
2	garlic cloves, minced	2
1 tsp	dried oregano	5 mL
½ tsp	dried basil	2 mL
¼ tsp	salt	1 mL
¼ tsp	pepper	1 mL
dash	crushed red pepper flakes	dash
2	plum tomatoes, chopped	2
½ cup	pitted Greek olives, chopped	125 mL
1 Tbsp	minced fresh parsley	15 mL

Directions:

1. In a small saucepan, bring water to a boil. Stir in barley. Reduce heat; cover and simmer for 10-12 minutes or until barley is tender. Remove from heat; let stand for 5 minutes.

2. Meanwhile, in a large skillet or wok, stir-fry chicken in 2 tsp (10 mL) canola oil until no longer pink. Remove and keep warm.

3. Stir-fry onion in 1 tsp (5 mL) canola oil for 3 minutes. Add the zucchini, garlic, oregano, basil, salt, pepper and pepper flakes; stir-fry for 2-4 minutes longer or until vegetables are crisp-tender. Add the chicken, tomatoes, olives and parsley. Serve with barley.

About This Recipe: This Mediterranean stir-fry has the perfect blend of Greek spices for a low-fat version of chicken souvlaki!

Per Serving: 423 kcal, 14 g fat, 2 g saturated fat, 44 g carbohydrate, 10 g fibre, 31 g protein.

Cook Once, Eat Twice or More: Tuck some of this recipe into a whole-wheat wrap for tomorrow's lunch. Or toss the vegetable-chicken mixture into whole-wheat pasta such as penne, instead of using the barley.

Orange-Glazed Salmon over Sautéed Spinach

Serves 4 - Serving Size: Approximately 3 oz (85 g) salmon

Ingredients:

1	orange, washed, grated* and juiced	1
2 Tbsp	honey	30 mL
1 Tbsp	brown sugar	15 mL
2 tsp	canola oil	10 mL
¼ tsp	red pepper flakes	1 mL
1	12 oz (340 g) salmon fillet, cut in 4 pieces	1
8 oz	fresh spinach, trimmed	250 g
1 tsp	canola oil	5 mL
1 Tbsp	lemon juice	15 mL
⅛ tsp	freshly-ground black pepper	0.5 mL

Directions:

1. Combine juice from orange, honey, brown sugar, 2 tsp (10 mL) canola oil and red pepper flakes.

2. Arrange salmon in dish just big enough to hold fillet; pour orange juice mixture over salmon. Marinate in refrigerator for 30 minutes, turning salmon once to distribute flavours. Discard marinade.

3. Grill salmon skin side up, over medium heat for 5-7 minutes; turn and cook for another 5-7 minutes, until fish flakes easily.

4. Just before salmon is done, sauté spinach in 1 tsp (5 mL) canola oil in non-stick skillet, just until wilted. Season with lemon juice and pepper.

5. Spoon spinach onto heated plates. Top with salmon. Sprinkle with grated orange peel.

* Reserve grated orange rind for garnish. Grate the orange prior to juicing.

About This Recipe: Sautéed spinach is an excellent source of vitamin A and provides great eye appeal to this dish.

Per Serving: 284 kcal, 11 g fat, 1 g saturated fat, 24 g carbohydrate, 4 g fibre, 24 g protein.

Healthy Tip: Salmon is a rich source of essential omega-3 fatty acids that prevent heart disease and stroke. A serving of salmon in this recipe also provides the amount of vitamin B$_{12}$ and vitamin D you need for the day.

Roasted Veggie, Fresh Veggie Salsa

Serves 8 – Serving Size ¼ cup (60 mL)

Ingredients:

1	medium yellow or orange bell pepper, diced	1
½	medium red onion, coarsely chopped	½
1	small zucchini, cut in half lengthwise and cut into ½-inch (1 cm) slices	1
1 Tbsp	canola oil	15 mL
1 cup	grape tomatoes, quartered	250 mL
1	medium garlic clove, minced	1
2 Tbsp	chopped fresh parsley or cilantro	30 mL
1 Tbsp	cider vinegar	15 mL
1 Tbsp	canola oil	15 mL
½ tsp	salt	2 mL
⅛ tsp	dried pepper flakes, optional	5 mL

Directions:

1. Preheat oven to 425°F (220°C).

2. Place the peppers, onions and zucchini on a foil-lined baking sheet. Spoon 1 Tbsp (15 mL) of the canola oil over all and toss to coat. Arrange in a single layer and bake for 15 minutes, stir and bake for an additional 5 minutes or until richly browned on edges. Remove from oven.

3. Pull the sides of the foil together and seal. Let stand 15 minutes to allow the juices to be released and to cool slightly.

4. Meanwhile, combine the remaining ingredients in a medium bowl.

5. Stir in the roasted vegetable mixture. Serve immediately for more pronounced flavours, or for a more blended flavour may serve within 8 hours.

About This Recipe: This versatile salsa can be used as an appetizer or as part of the main course!

Per Serving: 47 kcal, 4 g fat, 0.3 g saturated fat, 4 g carbohydrate, 1 g fibre, 1 g protein.

Cook Once, Eat Twice or More: This makes a great salsa or dip with pita chips, corn tortilla chips or crostini. It also makes a great topper for simple cuts of chicken, fish or pork.

Week 3, Day 3

Meal	Ingredients per Serving	Canada's Food Guide Servings
Breakfast Banana Raisin Wraps (recipe follows)	1 serving Banana Raisin Wraps 1 cup (250 mL) coffee / tea 2 Tbsp (30 mL) 1% milk (optional) 1 tsp (5 mL) granulated sugar (optional)	1 Vegetables and Fruit 1 Grains 1 Meat and Alternatives
Morning Snack Veggies with Hummus (see week 1)	¼ cup (60 mL) broccoli ¼ cup (60 mL) zucchini sticks 2 Tbsp (30 mL) hummus	1 Vegetables and Fruit ½ Meat and Alternatives
Lunch Warm Salmon Pasta Salad (recipe follows)	1 serving Warm Salmon Pasta Salad 1 apple 1 slice whole-wheat toast 1 cup (250 mL) 1% milk	2 ½ Vegetables and Fruit 2 Grain Products ½ Meat and Alternatives 1 Milk and Alternatives 1 Oils and Fats
Afternoon Snack Biscuits and Yogurt	4 arrowroot biscuits ¾ cup (175 mL) low-fat plain yogurt	1 Grain Products 1 Milk and Alternatives
Dinner Stovetop Shepherd's Pie (recipe follows)	1 serving Stovetop Shepherd's Pie 1 cup (250 mL) mixed greens 1 Tbsp (15 mL) each bell pepper, celery, dried cranberries, chopped pecans 1 Tbsp (15 mL) low-fat salad dressing	4 Vegetables and Fruit 1 Meat and Alternatives ½ Milk and Alternatives 1 Oils and Fats
Evening Snack Strawberry Bran Muffin and Milk (see week 2)	1 Strawberry Bran Muffin 1 cup (250 mL) 1% milk	1 Grain Products 1 Milk and Alternatives
Total Servings:		8 ½ Vegetables and Fruit 5 Grain Products 3 Meat and Alternatives 3 ½ Milk and Alternatives 2 Oils and Fats

Good To Know

Nutrition facts of the day	Adjusting today's menu
Calories: 2040 Fat: 76 g Saturated fat: 18 g Carbohydrate: 241 g Fibre: 33 g Protein: 109 g	*To cut about 200 calories* · Reduce hummus to 1 Tbsp (15 mL) at morning snack (saves 30 kcal) · Use half serving size of the dressing for the pasta salad (saves 65 kcal) · Reduce yogurt at afternoon snack to ½ cup (125 mL) and reduce arrowroot biscuits to two (saves 100 kcal) *To add about 200 calories* · Drink 1 cup (250 mL) 1% milk with your breakfast (adds 100 kcal) · Instead of biscuits, have ½ cup (125mL) low-fat granola with the yogurt for afternoon snack (adds 80 kcal) · Add an additional 1 Tbsp (15 mL) chopped pecans to the salad at dinner (adds 40 kcal)

Banana Raisin Wraps
Serves 4 - Serving Size: 1 wrap

Ingredients:

½ cup	peanut butter	125 mL
4	8-inch (20 cm) whole-wheat flour tortillas	4
2	medium firm bananas	2
½ cup	fresh fruit, such as strawberries	125 mL

Directions:

1. Spread peanut butter over one side of each tortilla.

2. Arrange banana pieces and sliced strawberries over peanut butter, press lightly.

3. Roll up loosely; cut in half.

About This Recipe: A quick on-the-go breakfast. Eating healthy can be easy, even for those busy mornings when you're rushing out the door.

Per Serving: 403 kcal, 20 g fat, 4 g saturated fat, 49 g carbohydrate, 7 g fibre, 13 g protein.

Healthy Tip: Pea butter is a great substitute for peanut butter and it's made right here in the Prairies!

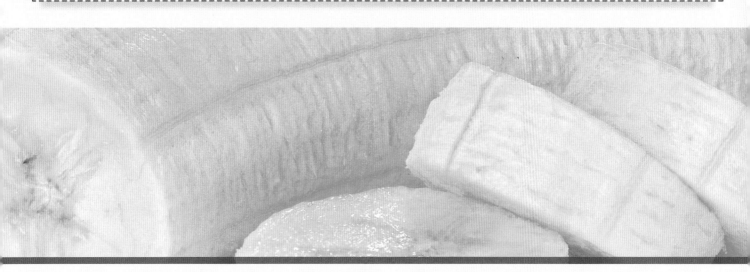

Warm Salmon Pasta Salad
Serves 4 - Serving Size: approximately 1 ½ cup (375 ml)

Ingredients:

1 cup	whole-wheat bow-tie pasta	250 mL
½	red apple, cored and diced	½
1 can	6 oz (170 g) sockeye salmon, drained, broken into bite-size pieces	1 can
½ cup	sliced celery	125 mL
1 ½	green onions, diced	1 ½
½	small zucchini, trimmed and diced	½
½	yellow pepper, seeded and diced	½
½ cup	frozen baby peas, thawed	125 mL

Curry vinaigrette:

¼ cup	canola oil	60 mL
1 ½ tsp	lemon juice	7 mL
1 tsp	curry powder pepper, to taste	5 mL
2 Tbsp	coarsely chopped walnuts	30 mL

Directions:

1. Cook pasta according to package directions. Drain well.

2. In a salad bowl, combine pasta, apple, salmon, celery, green onions, zucchini, yellow pepper and baby peas. Set aside.

3. To prepare the vinaigrette: in a small bowl, combine canola oil, lemon juice, curry powder, salt and pepper. Heat for 30 seconds in microwave.

4. Pour vinaigrette over salad and toss lightly. Garnish with walnuts. Serve immediately.

About This Recipe: A unique twist on the pasta salads that are often brought to potlucks and barbecues. Walnuts really add a unique flavour to this recipe. For a bit more colour, add fresh herbs like parsley when they're in season.

Per Serving: 352 kcal, 21 g fat, 2 g saturated fat, 22 g carbohydrate, 4 g fibre, 21 g protein.

Chef's Tip: You can use leftover salmon from last night instead of canned salmon if desired.

Stovetop Shepherd's Pie

Serves 4 - Serving Size: Approximately 2 cups (500 mL)

Ingredients:

1 lb	potatoes, peeled (if desired) and cut into ½-inch (1 cm) cubes	450 g
¾ cup	water	175 mL
½ cup	1% milk	125 mL
¼ tsp	salt	1 mL
	black pepper to taste	
1 Tbsp	canola oil	15 mL
1 lb	extra lean ground beef	450 g
1 ½ cups	diced onions	250 mL
¼ cup	diced green bell pepper	375 mL
¼ cup	ground flaxseed	60 mL
1 cup	tomato sauce	250 mL
1 Tbsp	Worcestershire sauce	15 mL
¼ tsp	salt	1 mL
1 oz	shredded regular sharp cheddar cheese	30 g

Directions:

1. Combine the potatoes and water in a medium saucepan over high heat, bring to a boil, reduce to medium, cover and simmer for 5 minutes or until potatoes are very tender. Remove from heat. Mash with a potato masher or fork, gradually stir in the milk. Mash until smooth and stir in ¼ tsp (1 mL) of the salt and black pepper, cover and set aside. (Note: potato mixture will be a bit "loose" at this point, but will thicken.)

2. Meanwhile, heat the canola oil in a large skillet over medium high heat. Cook the beef for 4 minutes or until browned, stirring frequently. Use a food thermometer to make sure your ground beef has a temperature of 160°F (70°C).

3. Add the onions and bell peppers to the beef and cook for 5 minutes or until tender-crisp.

4. Stir in the flaxseed until well blended. Stir in the tomato sauce and Worcestershire sauce.

5. Cover and cook on medium low heat for 10-12 minutes or until vegetables are tender, stirring occasionally.

6. Stir in remaining ¼ tsp (1 mL)of the salt. Spoon potatoes evenly over the beef mixture, sprinkle with the cheese, cover and cook for 5 minutes or until cheese has melted and potatoes have heated through.

About This Recipe: Ground flaxseed and canola oil are great sources of omega-3 fatty acids without altering the traditional flavour of this British-inspired dish.

Per Serving: 368 kcal, 12 g fat, 4 g saturated fat, 38 g carbohydrate, 8 g fibre, 32 g protein.

Week 3, Day 4

Meal	Ingredients per Serving	Canada's Food Guide Servings
Breakfast Whole-wheat Bagel with Peanut Butter and Cream Cheese	1 small whole-wheat bagel 1 Tbsp (15 mL) low-fat cream cheese 1 Tbsp (15 mL) peanut butter 1 orange 1 cup (250 mL) coffee / tea 2 Tbsp (30 mL) 1% milk (optional) 1 tsp (5 mL) granulated sugar (optional)	1 Vegetables and Fruit 2 Grain Products ½ Meat and Alternatives
Morning Snack Egg Salad Sandwich	1 chopped hardboiled egg 1 slice whole-wheat bread 2 Tbsp (30 mL) low-fat mayonnaise 2 Tbsp (30 mL) red onion	¼ Vegetables and Fruit 1 Grain Products ½ Meat and Alternatives 2 Oils and Fats
Lunch Cucumber and Black Bean Salsa Salad (recipe follows)	1 serving Cucumber and Black Bean Salsa Salad ½ baked whole-wheat pita 1 cup (250 mL) 1% milk	2 Vegetables and Fruit 1 Grain Products ½ Meat and Alternatives 1 Milk and Alternatives 1 Oils and Fats
Afternoon Snack Roasted Almonds with Pretzels	¼ cup (60 mL) roasted almonds ½ oz (15 g) pretzels	1 Grain Products 1 Meat and Alternatives
Dinner Vegetarian Cabbage Rolls with Healthy Borscht Soup (recipes follow)	1 serving Vegetarian Cabbage Rolls 1 serving Healthy Borscht Soup 1 whole-wheat dinner roll 1 tsp (5 mL) non-hydrogenated margarine ½ cup (125 mL) 1% milk	6 ½ Vegetables and Fruit 1 ½ Grain Products ½ Milk and Alternatives 1 Oils and Fats
Evening Snack Fruit Yogurt and Cereal	¾ cup (175 mL) low-fat fruit yogurt ½ cup (125 mL) cereal (e.g., Cheerios)	½ Grain Products 1 Milk and Alternatives
Total Servings:		9 ¾ Vegetables and Fruit 7 Grain Products 2 ½ Meat and Alternatives 2 ½ Milk and Alternatives 4 Oils and Fats

Good To Know

Nutrition facts of the day	Adjusting today's menu
Calories: 2150 Fat: 70 g Saturated fat: 15 g Carbohydrate: 316 g Fibre: 46 g Protein: 94 g	*To cut about 200 calories* · Add only 1 Tbsp (15 mL) mayonnaise to the egg salad (saves 35 kcal) · Reduce almonds to 2 Tbsp (30 mL) at afternoon snack (saves 80 kcal) · Skip margarine and milk at dinner (saves 115 kcal) *To add about 200 calories* · Drink ½ cup (125 mL) 1% milk with breakfast (adds 50 kcal) · Add an apple to morning snack (adds 95 kcal) · Have 2 Tbsp (30 mL) hummus with the pita bread at lunch (adds 50 kcal)

Cucumber and Black Bean Salsa Salad

Serves 4 - Serving Size: Approximately 1 ½ cups (375 mL)

Ingredients:

1	large cucumber, diced	1
1 cup	grape or cherry tomatoes, halved	250 mL
1 can	15 oz (443 mL) black beans, rinsed and drained	1 can
¼ cup	red onion, finely chopped	60 mL
1	medium green bell pepper, seeded and diced	1
1	medium jalapeno, seeded and minced, optional	1
¼ cup	fresh cilantro leaves, chopped	60 mL
1	medium lime (grated peel and juiced)	1
2 tsp	cider vinegar	10 mL
1 Tbsp	canola oil	15 mL
¼ tsp	pepper	1 mL

Directions:

1. Put all ingredients in a bowl.

2. Toss gently and thoroughly to blend. Serve immediately or cover and refrigerate up to 4 hours to blend flavours.

 About This Recipe: The black beans give this salad a boost of fibre, protein, and iron! The jalapeno, lime and cilantro recreate authentic Mexican flavours.

Per Serving: 132 kcal, 4 g fat, 0.3 g saturated fat, 24 g carbohydrate, 8 g fibre, 6 g protein.

 Healthy Tip: This versatile, healthy salad contains more than 8 grams of fibre per serving! To get your daily orange vegetable serving, top this salad with ½ cup (125 mL) grated carrot. (Grate enough to use later in the cabbage rolls). Add the salad to a chicken wrap for lunch or serve it as a side for dinner.

Vegetarian Cabbage Rolls
Serves 6 - Serving Size: 2 cabbage rolls

Ingredients:

10 cups	water	2.5 L
½ tsp	salt	2 mL
1	5 lb (2.2 kg) cabbage	1
1 ½ tsp	canola oil	7 mL
1	onion, chopped	1
1	clove garlic, minced	1
1 tsp	dried marjoram or dried oregano	5 mL
½ tsp	dried thyme	2 mL
¼ tsp	caraway seeds, crushed (optional)	1 mL
1 cup	long grain white rice	250 mL
2 cups	low-sodium vegetable broth	500 mL
1	carrot, grated	1
1	zucchini, grated	1
¼ tsp	salt	1 mL
¼ tsp	pepper	1 mL
1	egg, beaten	1
1 can	28 oz (796 mL) sauerkraut, rinsed and drained	1
¼ cup	tomato paste	60 mL
2 ½ cups	tomato juice	625 mL

Directions:

1. Preheat oven to 350°F (180°C), and bring a pot of salted water to a boil.

2. Remove core from cabbage. In large pot of boiling salted water, cover and cook cabbage for 8-10 minutes or until leaves are softened and easy to remove. Remove from the boiling water and immerse immediately in cold water to chill and stop cooking process. Carefully remove 12 leaves, returning cabbage to boiling water for 2-3 minutes if leaves become difficult to remove. Drain individual leaves on towels. Pare off coarse veins; set leaves aside.

3. In saucepan, heat canola oil over medium heat; cook onion, garlic, marjoram, thyme, and caraway seeds (if using) for 5 minutes or until softened. Stir in rice. Add broth and bring to a boil; reduce heat, cover and simmer for 20 minutes or until rice is tender. Stir in carrot, zucchini, salt and pepper.

4 Let cool to room temperature. Stir in egg. Spoon about ⅓ cup (75 mL) of mixture onto each leaf just above stem. Fold sides, then bottom over filling; roll up.

5. Line 13 x 9 inch (22 x 33 cm) baking dish with half of the sauerkraut. Arrange cabbage rolls on top; cover with remaining sauerkraut. Whisk tomato paste into tomato juice; pour over rolls. Cover with foil; bake in a 350°F (180°C) oven for 2 hours or until tender.

* Rinse sauerkraut before using. It can be quite sour and salty.

About This Recipe: Even carnivores will be surprised at how tasty these cabbage rolls are! Marjoram, thyme, and caraway pack in the flavour.

Per Serving: 350 kcal, 3 g fat, 0.6 g saturated fat, 75 g carbohydrate, 12 g fibre, 10 g protein.

Healthy Borscht Soup
Serves 14 – Serving Size 1 cup (250 mL)

Ingredients:

2	medium onions, chopped	2
1 cup	diced carrots	250 mL
1 cup	diced celery	250 mL
1 cup	shredded cabbage	250 mL
3 Tbsp	canola oil	45 mL
1 cup	peeled and diced potatoes	250 mL
2 cups	peeled and diced beets	500 mL
6 ½ cups	water	1.5 L
1 cup	low sodium tomato juice	250 mL
2 cups	low sodium vegetable broth	500 mL
1 Tbsp	lemon juice	15 mL
2	bay leaves	2
1 tsp	salt	5 mL
	fresh dill and parsley (to taste)	
14 Tbsp	low-fat or fat-free sour cream	210 mL

Directions:

1. In a large soup pot, sauté onion, carrot, celery and cabbage in canola oil until cooked.

2. Add potatoes and beets and continue to sauté for about one minute.

3. Add water, tomato juice and broth. Season with lemon juice, bay leaves and salt. Allow to simmer until potatoes are cooked, about 15-20 minutes.

4. Add dill and parsley near the end of the cooking time for maximum flavour impact.

5. Remove from heat. Remove bay leaves and serve. Garnish each bowl with 1 Tbsp (15 mL) low-fat or fat-free sour cream, if desired.

About This Recipe: This traditional Ukrainian dish has a deep red-purple colour, and may be served hot or cold.

Per Serving: 63 kcal, 3 g fat, 0.3 g saturated fat, 8 g carbohydrate, 2 g fibre, 1 g protein.

Cook Once, Eat Twice or More: This colourful soup can also be frozen for up to 3 months, for later enjoyment!

Meal	Ingredients per Serving	Canada's Food Guide Servings
Breakfast Fruity Breakfast Oats (recipe follows)	1 serving Fruity Breakfast Oats ½ cup (125 mL) 1% milk 1 cup (250 mL) coffee / tea 2 Tbsp (30 mL) 1% milk (optional) 1 tsp (5 mL) granulated sugar (optional)	2 Vegetables and Fruit 1 Grain Products ½ Meat and Alternatives ½ Milk and Alternatives
Morning Snack Sweet-Spiced Carrot Muffins (recipe follows)	½ Sweet-Spiced Carrot Muffin ½ cup (125 mL) 1% milk	½ Grain Products ½ Milk and Alternatives
Lunch Tuna Open-Faced Sandwiches with Bacon (recipe follows)	1 serving Tuna Open-Faced Sandwich with Bacon ½ cup (125 mL) 1% milk	4 ¼ Vegetables and Fruit 1 Grain Products 1 ½ Meat and Alternatives ½ Milk and Alternatives 1 Oils and Fats
Afternoon Snack Chili Popcorn with Milk (recipe follows)	1 serving Chili Popcorn ½ cup (125 mL) 1% milk	½ Grain Products ½ Milk and Alternatives ½ Oils and Fats
Dinner Chicken with Lime, Garlic and Cashews (recipe follows)	1 serving Chicken with Lime, Garlic and Cashews ¾ cup (175 mL) cooked brown rice ½ cup (125 mL) 1% milk	1 Vegetables and Fruit 1 ½ Grain Products ¾ Meat and Alternatives ½ Milk and Alternatives ½ Oils and Fats
Evening Snack Banana and Cranberry Bread Pudding (recipe follows)	1 serving Banana and Cranberry Bread Pudding	¼ Vegetables and Fruit 1 Grain Products ¼ Milk and Alternatives
Total Servings:		7 ½ Vegetables and Fruit 5 ½ Grain Products 2 ¾ Meat and Alternatives 2 ¾ Milk and Alternatives 2 Oils and Fats

Good To Know

Nutrition facts of the day	Adjusting today's menu
Calories: 1823 Fat: 52 g Saturated fat: 14 g Carbohydrate: 260 g Fibre: 22 g Protein: 85 g	*To cut about 200 calories* · Skip sour cream in the sandwich at lunch (saves 30 kcal) · Skip the brown rice at dinner (saves 160 kcal) *To add about 200 calories* · Add another piece of toast to the sandwich at lunch (adds 70 kcal) · Mix 2 Tbsp (30 mL) chopped almonds into the popcorn at afternoon snack (adds 65 kcal) · Increase milk to 1 cup (250 mL) at dinner (adds 50 kcal)

Fruity Breakfast Oats
Serves 4 - Serving Size: Approximately 2 cups (500 mL)

Ingredients:

1 cup	quick-cooking rolled oats	250 mL
½ cup	milk	125 mL
1 ½ cups	low-fat fruit yogurt	375 mL
¼ cup	maple syrup	60 mL
1	red apple, peeled and grated	1
1	ripe pear, peeled and chopped	1
2 cups	mixed berries, fresh or frozen, thawed	500 mL
½ cup	chopped almonds (or other nuts), toasted	125 mL

Directions:

1. Combine oats, milk, yogurt, maple syrup, apple and pear together in a large bowl. Mixture can be covered and left overnight in the refrigerator at this stage.

2. Add berries and almonds and gently stir to combine. Serve immediately.

About This Recipe: Oatmeal offers a source of unrefined whole grains, combined with a source of calcium from the milk and yogurt!

Per Serving: 424 kcal, 12 g fat, 2 saturated fat, 70 g carbohydrate, 8 g fibre, 13 g protein.

Healthy Tip: Try this easy breakfast with your favourite dried fruits, or a combination of dried and fresh to take advantage of what you have on hand.

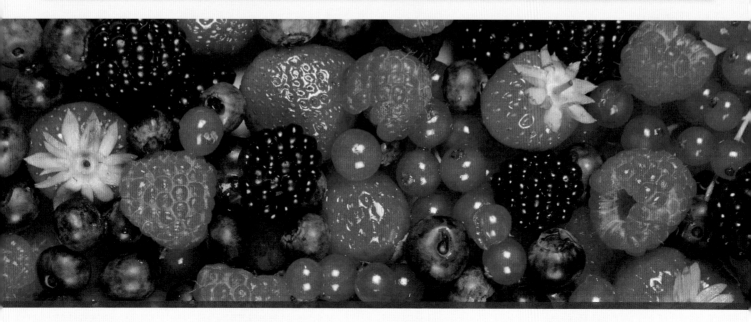

Sweet-Spiced Carrot Muffins

Serves 18 - Serving Size: 1 muffin

Ingredients:

	canola oil cooking spray	
¾ cup	all-purpose flour	175 mL
½ cup	whole-wheat flour	125 mL
1 cup	quick cooking oats	250 mL
½ cup	packed brown sugar	125 mL
2 tsp	baking powder	10 mL
1 ½ tsp	ground cinnamon	7 mL
¼ tsp	salt	1 mL
½ cup	1% milk	125 mL
⅓ cup	canola oil	75 mL
1	large egg	1
1 ½ cups	shredded carrots, about 3 medium	375 mL
1 cup	diced apple	250 mL
½ cup	pecan pieces, chopped	125 mL
⅓ cup	raisins	75 mL
⅓ cup	sweetened flaked coconut	75 mL

Directions:

1. Preheat oven to 350°F (180°C). Lightly spray two non-stick 12-cup muffin pans with canola oil cooking spray.

2. Whisk together flours, oats, sugar, baking powder, cinnamon and salt in a large bowl. Make a well in centre of mixture.

3. Whisk together the milk, oil and egg in a medium bowl; add the carrots, apple, pecans, raisins and coconut. Stir until well blended.

4. Stir into the flour mixture until just blended. Do not over mix. Spoon batter into 18 of the prepared muffin cups.

5. Bake 17-18 minutes or until wooden toothpick inserted comes out clean. Place muffin pans on wire racks and let stand for 5 minutes before removing.

6. Place muffins on a wire rack to cool completely. Store in an airtight container. As with most baked items with fruit, flavours and texture improve overnight.

About This Recipe: These muffins contain a source of vitamin A from the carrots! They're the perfect snack to microwave when you're on the run.

Per Serving: 162 kcal, 8 g fat, 1 g saturated fat, 22 g carbohydrate, 2 g fibre, 3 g protein.

Chef's Tip: For a softer raisin, combine ½ cup (125 mL) boiling water and the raisins and let stand for 5 minutes. Drain, discarding liquid, and add the raisins to the batter.

Tuna Open-Faced Sandwiches with Bacon

Serves 4 - Serving Size: ½ cup (125 mL) tuna salad

Ingredients:

2 cans	6 oz (170 g) tuna packed in water, rinsed and well drained	2 cans
⅓ cup	low-fat canola mayonnaise	75 mL
¼ cup	low-fat sour cream	60 mL
2 Tbsp	1% milk	30 mL
4 tsp	granulated sugar	20 mL
1 cup	diced celery	250 mL
4	whole-wheat bread slices, toasted	4
4	bacon slices, cooked and crumbled	4
1 cup	fresh spinach leaves	250 mL
1	large tomato, cut into 4 slices	1

Directions:

1. Combine the tuna, mayonnaise, sour cream, milk and sugar in a medium bowl, stir until well blended. Stir in the celery.

2. Top each piece of toast with equal amounts of the spinach and tomatoes. Spoon equal amounts of the tuna on top of the tomatoes and sprinkle evenly with the bacon.

 About This Recipe: Tuna is an excellent source of lean protein. Spinach and tomatoes give these sandwiches a boost of vitamin C.

Per Serving: 314 kcal, 13 g fat, 4 g saturated fat, 22 g carbohydrate, 3 g fibre, 25 g protein.

 Healthy Tip: To decrease the total fat of the recipe, substitute turkey bacon and use ½ cup (125 mL) fat-free Greek yogurt instead of mayonnaise and sour cream.

Chili Popcorn
Serves 12 - Serving Size: 1 cup (250 mL)

Ingredients:

3 quarts	popped popcorn (about 12 cups)	3 L
2 Tbsp	butter or non-hydrogenated margarine, melted	30 mL
1 Tbsp	Dijon mustard	15 mL
2 Tbsp	chili powder	30 mL
¼ tsp	salt	1 mL
¼ tsp	ground cumin	1 mL

Directions:

1. Place popcorn in a large bowl.

2. Combine the remaining ingredients. Drizzle over popcorn. Toss until well coated.

 About This Recipe: With the use of herbs and spices, your popcorn on family movie night will never be the same!
Per Serving: 53 kcal, 2 g fat, 0.4 g saturated fat (when made with margarine), 7 g carbohydrate, 2 g fibre, 1 g protein.

 Healthy Tip: Homemade popcorn is a low-fat, low-calorie snack; 2 cups (500 mL) is equal to one grain product serving according to the Canada's Food Guide. Two cups of popcorn contains 2.3 grams of fibre. Experiment with different herbs and spices to replace the salt.

Chicken with Lime, Garlic and Cashews

Serves 4 - Serving Size: Approximately 1 ½ cups (375 mL)

Ingredients:

1	**7 oz (200 g) boneless, skinless chicken breast**	1
4	**cloves garlic, minced**	4
2 Tbsp	**low-sodium soy sauce**	30 mL
2 Tbsp	**garlic chili sauce**	30 mL
1 tsp	**canola oil**	5 mL
2 tsp	**fresh lime juice**	10 mL
1 tsp	**canola oil**	5 mL
2	**large red peppers, thinly sliced**	2
1 cup	**snap or snow peas**	250 mL
6	**green onions, chopped into 4-inch (10 cm) pieces**	6
¼ cup	**unsalted cashews, chopped coarsely**	60 mL

Directions:

1. Slice the chicken into ¼-inch (5mm) slices. For easier slicing, place chicken in freezer for 20 minutes to firm.

2. In resealable plastic bag, mix together garlic, soy sauce, chili sauce, 1 tsp (5 mL) canola oil and lime juice. Add sliced chicken. Marinate in refrigerator for 20 minutes to 12 hours.

3. When chicken is marinated, heat medium frying pan over medium heat. Add 1 tsp (5 mL) canola oil and red peppers. Sauté for 1 minute. Remove peppers from pan and set aside on a plate.

4. Add chicken with marinade to frying pan. Stir-fry chicken for 4 minutes. Return red peppers to pan and continue cooking for 1 minute. Add snow peas and green onions and cook for 2 minutes. Sprinkle with cashews and stir-fry for 1 minute. Serve.

About This Recipe: Marinating chicken is a great way to try new flavours by altering herbs and spices. Garlic, chilies, and soy sauce give prairie chicken extra flavour - with an Asian twist.

Per Serving: 198 kcal, 8 g fat, 2 g saturated fat, 17 g carbohydrate, 3 g fibre, 14 g protein.

Quick Tip: Prepare the chicken in the morning or the night before and your dinner is ready in a few minutes! The longer you let the chicken marinate, the bolder your flavour will be. Red pepper in this recipe gives you the daily requirement of vitamin C.

Banana and Cranberry Bread Pudding

Serves 6 - Serving Size: 1 slice

Ingredients:

6 slices	raisin cinnamon bread	6 slices
¼ cup	dried cranberries or raisins	60 mL
½	small orange (zest and juice)	½
¾ cup	low-fat milk	175 mL
2	eggs	2
½ cup	low-fat vanilla yogurt	125 mL
2 Tbsp	brown sugar	30 mL
¾ tsp	cinnamon	4 mL
¼ tsp	nutmeg	1 mL
½ tsp	vanilla	2 mL
1 ½	ripe bananas	1 ½

Sauce:

1 Tbsp	honey	15 mL
½ cup	low-fat vanilla yogurt	125 mL

Directions:
Bread Pudding:

1. Preheat oven to 350°F (180°C).

2. Lightly butter an 8 x 8 inch (20 cm x 20 cm) baking dish and set aside.

3. Cut the raisin cinnamon bread into cubes and place in a large bowl. Add dried cranberries (or raisins) and orange zest and set aside.

4. Prepare custard by beating together milk, eggs, yogurt, brown sugar, orange juice, cinnamon, nutmeg and vanilla.

5. Mash bananas in a separate bowl and set aside.

6. Pour custard mixture over the bread. Mix well and let stand for 15 minutes until liquid is well absorbed. Mix bananas into bread and custard mixture. Pour into baking dish. Place in centre of oven and bake for 50-65 minutes.

7. Test for doneness by inserting a toothpick into the center of the pudding. The toothpick will come out clean when the bread pudding is ready to serve. Cut into 6 slices.

Sauce:

1. Warm the honey in a small sauce pan on low heat.

2. Remove from heat and mix the yogurt into the honey.

3. Spoon over warm bread pudding and serve.

About This Recipe: The bananas in this pudding are a great source of potassium, which is a mineral essential for maintaining proper fluid balance.

Per Serving: 405 kcal, 7 g fat, 3 g saturated fat, 75 g carbohydrate, 3 g dietary fibre, 11 g protein.

Head to Head: How the Nutrients Stack Up

Cooking and Salad Oils: Types of fat in grams / Tbsp

Fat	Canola	Olive	Safflower	Corn	Coconut
Saturated	0.9	1.8	0.8	1.7	11.8
Monounsaturated	8.2	10.0	10.2	3.3	0.8
Polyunsaturated	4.1	1.2	2.0	8.0	0.2
Trans	0.0	0.0	0.0	0.0	0.0

In October 2006, the US Food and Drug Administration authorized a Qualified Health Claim for canola oil based on its high percentage of unsaturated fats. Polyunsaturated and monounsaturated fats from vegetable oils help lower cholesterol. The polyunsaturated fat found in canola oil includes alpha linolenic acid (ALA), an essential omega-3 fatty acid.

Tips for Healthier Salads

Commercial salad dressings may be a significant source of salt. To make your own low-salt salad dressing, whisk 2 Tbsp (30 mL) canola or olive oil with 1 Tbsp (15 mL) vinegar of your choice and 1 Tbsp (15 mL) water. Add 1 tsp (5 mL) Dijon mustard, 1-2 tsp (5-10 mL) of herbs (such as Italian seasoning, tarragon or rosemary) and ¼ tsp (1 mL) black pepper. Store in a jar with a tight lid. This recipe may be doubled or tripled, depending on your needs. One serving of 1 Tbsp (15 mL) contains 61 kcal, 6.9 g fat (0.5 g saturated fat) and 15 mg sodium.

Compare this with 1 serving of commercial regular Italian salad dressing, which contains 43 calories, 4.2 g fat (0.7 g saturated fat) and a whopping 243 mg sodium as well as 1.2 g sugar. Low calorie Italian dressing has only 11 kcal and 1 g fat, but still has 205 mg sodium and 0.7 g sugar. *(Source: Dietitians of Canada)*

Week 3, Day 6

Meal	Ingredients per Serving	Canada's Food Guide Servings
Breakfast Strawberry Banana Yogurt Parfait	¾ cup (175 mL) low-fat fruit vanilla or strawberry yogurt ½ banana ½ cup (125 mL) strawberries, fresh or frozen 1 slice whole-wheat toast 1 tsp (5 mL) non-hydrogenated margarine 1 cup (250 mL) coffee / tea 2 Tbsp (30 mL) 1% milk (optional) 1 tsp (5 mL) granulated sugar (optional)	1 Vegetables and Fruit 1 Grain Products 1 Milk and Alternatives 1 Oils and Fats
Morning Snack Rice Cakes with Milk	2 rice cakes ½ cup (125 mL) 1% milk	1 Grain Products ½ Milk and Alternatives
Lunch Chicken Noodle Bowl (recipe follows)	1 serving Chicken Noodle Bowl	3 ½ Vegetables and Fruit ½ Grain Products 1 Meat and Alternatives ¼ Milk and Alternatives 1 Oils and Fats
Afternoon Snack Tortilla Wrap with Yogurt	½ whole-wheat tortilla 2 Tbsp (30 mL) hummus ½ cup (125 mL) fresh / roasted red pepper ½ cup (125 mL) low-fat plain yogurt	1 Vegetables and Fruit 1 Grain Products ¾ Milk and Alternatives
Dinner Garlic-Pepper Tenderloin Steak with Roasted Vegetables with Herbs (recipes follow)	1 serving Garlic-Pepper Tenderloin Steak 1 serving Roasted Vegetables with Herbs 1 whole-wheat dinner roll 1 tsp (5 mL) non-hydrogenated margarine	2 ½ Vegetables and Fruit 1 Grain Products 1 ½ Meat and Alternatives 1 ½ Oils and Fats
Evening Snack Berry Citrus Brown Betty (recipe follows)	1 serving Berry Citrus Brown Betty ½ cup (125 mL) low-fat vanilla yogurt	1 Vegetables and Fruit 1 Grain Products ¾ Milk and Alternatives
Total Servings:		9 Vegetables and Fruit 5 ½ Grain Products 2 ½ Meat and Alternatives 3 ¼ Milk and Alternatives 3 ½ Oils and Fats

Good To Know

Nutrition facts of the day	Adjusting today's menu
Calories: 2052 Fat: 61 g Saturated fat: 17 g Carbohydrate: 272 g Fibre: 25 g Protein: 112 g	*To cut about 200 calories* · Skip ½ banana at breakfast (saves 50 kcal) · Skip red bell pepper at afternoon snack (saves 25 kcal) · Cut serving size of evening snack in half (saves 90 kcal) *To add about 200 calories* · Spread rice cakes with 1 Tbsp (15 mL) peanut butter at morning snack (adds 90 kcal) · Add a slice of whole-wheat toast to lunch (adds 70 kcal) · Add 1 cup (250 mL) milk at dinner (adds 100 kcal)

Chicken Noodle Bowl
Serves 4 - Serving Size: Approximately 1 ½ cups (375 mL)

Ingredients:

1 Tbsp	butter	15 mL
12 oz	boneless chicken breast (about 2 cut into thin strips)	340 g
2 Tbsp	minced fresh gingerroot or 1 tsp (5 mL) ground ginger	30 mL
3 cups	low-sodium chicken broth	750 mL
¼ cup	low-sodium soy sauce	60 mL
2 Tbsp	rice vinegar	30 mL
1 tsp	Asian red chili sauce, or to taste	5 mL
8 oz	small mushrooms, thinly sliced	225 g
3	celery stalks, thinly sliced	3
6 oz	wide rice noodles	170 g
2 Tbsp	cornstarch	30 mL
1 ½ cups	1% milk	375 mL
1 cup	bean sprouts	250 mL
2	green onions, thinly sliced	2

Directions:

1. Heat a large pot over medium-high heat. Add butter; swirl to coat. Add half each of the chicken and ginger and sauté for 2 minutes or until chicken is no longer pink inside; transfer to a bowl (some ginger will stick to pot). Repeat with remaining chicken and ginger. Set aside.

2. Add broth, soy sauce, vinegar and chili sauce to pot; increase heat to high and bring to boil, scraping up brown bits. Stir in mushrooms, celery and noodles. Whisk cornstarch into milk; stir into pot. Reduce heat to medium and cook, stirring, for 5-10 minutes or until bubbling and noodles are tender.

3. Stir in chicken mixture. Season to taste with chili sauce. Using tongs, divide chicken and noodles among warmed serving bowls; ladle broth on top. Top with bean sprouts and green onions.

About This Recipe: A hearty, low-sodium version of Vietnamese pho soup. For those who crave the heat, add as much red chili sauce as you can handle!

Per serving: 411 kcal, 8 g fat, 3.5 g saturated fat, 53 g carbohydrate, 2.4 g fibre, 31 g protein.

Quick Tip: Rice noodles are found at the asian food aisle in the grocery store. If they are not available, use other types of pasta instead.

Garlic-Pepper Tenderloin Steaks

Serves 4 - Serving Size: 4 oz (115 g) steak

Ingredients:

1 ½ tsp	minced garlic	7 mL
1 tsp	dried mustard	5 mL
1 tsp	paprika	5 mL
1 tsp	chili powder	5 mL
1 tsp	pepper	5 mL
½ tsp	salt	2 mL
½ tsp	dried thyme	2 mL
¼ tsp	cayenne pepper	1 mL
4	4 oz (115 g) beef tenderloin steaks	4
2 tsp	canola or olive oil	10 mL

Directions:

1. In a small bowl, combine seasonings. Brush steaks with oil; rub in seasoning mixture. Cover and refrigerate for at least 1 hour.

2. Using long-handled tongs, moisten a paper towel with cooking oil and lightly coat the grill rack.

3. Grill steaks, uncovered, over medium heat or broil 4-inches (10 cm) from the heat for 7-10 minutes on each side or until meat reaches desired doneness. For medium rare, a thermometer should read 145°F (63°C); medium, 160°F; and well-done, 170°F (77°C).

 About This Recipe: Who doesn't love a dinner hot off the grill? For cold days when you can't grill outdoors, an electric indoor grill will work just fine!

Per Serving: 280 kcal, 15 g fat, 5 g saturated fat, 2 g carbohydrate, 1 g fibre, 32 g protein.

 Healthy Tip: Be sure to trim any excess fat from the beef before preparing this dish.

 Quick Tip: Place leftover beef with roasted vegetables (see next recipe) into a whole-wheat pita and tomorrow's lunch is ready!

Roasted Vegetables with Herbs

Serves 4 - Serving Size: Approximately 1 cup (250 mL)

Ingredients:

5 cups	mixed vegetables such as potatoes, bell pepper, carrots, yams, red onion, zucchini, parsnip, turnip - chopped into ¾-inch (2 cm) squares	1.25 L
6	cloves garlic	6
2 Tbsp	canola oil	30 mL
2 Tbsp	balsamic or red wine vinegar	30 mL
1 tsp	mixed dried herbs, such as oregano, rosemary or thyme	5 mL

Directions:

1. Preheat oven to 425°F (220°C), and line a baking tray with parchment paper.

3. Toss garlic with vegetables, canola oil, vinegar and herbs.

2. Place all vegetables in a single layer on the baking tray.

4. Bake for 45-50 minutes or until golden. Toss every 15 minutes.

About This Recipe: Garlic and various herbs can transform any vegetable dish into a flavour-packed meal. Kids will forget they ever hated vegetables.

Per Serving: 169 kcal, 7 g fat, 0.6 g saturated fat, 24 g carbohydrate, 4 g fibre, 3 g protein.

Quick Tip: Serve this recipe as a bed for meats such as pork, lamb, chicken and turkey.

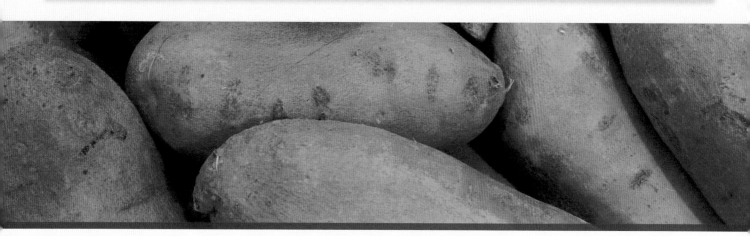

Berry Citrus Brown Betty
Serves 8 - Serving Size: ½ cup (125 mL)

Ingredients:

5 slices	whole-wheat bread, toasted	5 slices
½ cup	granulated sugar	125 mL
¾ tsp	ground cinnamon	4 mL
1 tsp	grated orange zest or grated ginger	5 mL
⅓ cup	orange juice or apple juice	100 mL
1 ½ cups	fresh or frozen, thawed raspberries	375 mL
1 ½ cups	fresh or frozen, thawed Saskatoon berries or blueberries	375 mL
1 cup	diced pears	250 mL
2 Tbsp	canola oil	30 mL
1 ½ Tbsp	butter or non-hydrogenated margarine, melted	25 mL

Directions:

1. Preheat the oven to 350°F (180°C).

2. Finely cut toast or tear toast pieces into 1 inch (2.5 cm) pieces; place bread cubes in food processor and pulse to coarse crumb texture.

3. In a small bowl, combine the sugar, cinnamon and zest.

4. Coat a shallow 2-quart baking dish with cooking spray. Place ⅓ of the crumbs (about 1 cup) in the bottom.

5. Sprinkle half of the pears and berries over the breadcrumbs, Sprinkle with half of the sugar mixture. Spoon the juice evenly over all.

6. Repeat with ⅓ of the breadcrumbs and the remaining fruit. Sprinkle the remaining breadcrumbs on top.

7. Drizzle the oil and butter or margarine evenly over all and sprinkle with the remaining sugar mixture.

8. Bake, uncovered, for 25 minutes. Cover with foil and bake for 15 minutes or until pears are tender and juices are bubbling.

9. Place on a wire rack and let stand for 30 minutes uncovered.

 About This Recipe: The perfect fruity dish for an evening treat or even breakfast on the go - just add low-fat yogurt! Use whatever fruit is in season.

Per Serving (with margarine): 187 kcal, 6 g fat, 0.7 g saturated fat, 31 g carbohydrate, 4 g fibre, 3 g protein.

About Cereal Grains

Eating Well with Canada's Food Guide recommends that at least half of your daily Grain Products choices comes from whole grains. It also recommends making sure that the grain products chosen are low in fat, sugar and salt.

Canada is one of the major grain growing and exporting countries in the world. Saskatchewan, Alberta and Manitoba produce 90% of the wheat grown in Canada. Most wheat is milled into flour. The prairie provinces also produce barley, oats, rye and triticale.

Grain Product	Use in Food Products	Nutritional Information (per 100 g)	Did you know?
Wheat	Flours, which are then used in baked goods, pasta and many other products. Wheat bran can be purchased separately.	Whole-Wheat Flour - 369 kcal, 3 g fat, 69 g carbohydrate, 9 g fibre, 15 g protein White Flour - 366 kcal, 2 g fat, 72 g carbohydrate, 3 g fibre, 12 g protein	Nearly half of all the wheat grown in Canada is in Saskatchewan. According to historical records, wheat was the first grain grown in Manitoba.
Barley	Noodles, breakfast cereals, baby formula, ingredient in soups and other products	Pearled Barley - 352 kcal, 1 g fat, 78 g carbohydrate, 16 g fibre, 10 g protein	About one-third to one-half of the fibre in barley is soluble, which gives it a low glycemic index.
Rye	Flours for rye bread, pumpernickel and crackers	Medium Rye Flour - 354 kcal, 2 g fat, 77 g carbohydrate, 15 g fibre, 9 g protein	Growing rye as a crop was introduced to Western Canada by Eastern European immigrants in the early 20th Century. Rye whiskey is known around the world as a Canadian product.
Oats	A versatile grain - porridge, breakfast cereal, cookies and snacks. Oat bran can be purchased separately.	Quick Oats (oatmeal) - 388 kcal, 7 g fat, 67 g carbohydrate, 9 g fibre, 13 g protein	Oats have been grown in Canada for 400 years. Instant oats cook more quickly than quick oats but have less fibre.
Triticale	Flour, breakfast cereal	Flour - 338 kcal, 2 g fat, 73 g carbohydrate, 15 g fibre, 13 g protein	Triticale is a hybrid of wheat (Triticum) and rye (Secale). Grown in Alberta Manitoba and Saskatchewan.

Week 3, Day 7

Meal	Ingredients per Serving	Canada's Food Guide Servings
Breakfast Garden Fresh Frittata (recipe follows)	1 serving Garden Fresh Frittata 1 slice whole-wheat toast 1 tsp (5 mL) margarine 1 cup (250 mL) 1% milk 1 cup (250 mL) coffee / tea 2 Tbsp (30 mL) 1% milk (optional) 1 tsp (5 mL) granulated sugar (optional)	¾ Vegetables and Fruit 1 Grain Products ¾ Meat and Alternatives 1 Milk and Alternatives 1 Oils and Fats
Morning Snack Cracker Melts (recipe follows)	1 serving Cracker Melts	1 Grain Products ½ Milk and Alternatives
Lunch Roast Beef Salad Pita	1 whole-wheat pita 2 Tbsp (30 mL) each red bell pepper, celery ¼ cup (60 mL) each baby carrots, red onion, zucchini 1 ½ garlic cloves 1 cup (250 mL) Romaine lettuce or spinach 1 oz (30 g) beef tenderloin steak (leftover) 1 tsp (5 mL) balsamic vinegar 2 tsp (10 mL) canola oil	3 Vegetables and Fruit 2 Grain Products ½ Meat and Alternatives 2 Oils and Fats
Afternoon Snack Purple Dinosaur and Melba Toast (recipe follows)	1 serving Purple Dinosaur 6 Melba toast	1 Grain Products 1 ½ Milk and Alternatives
Dinner Three-Way Chicken Kabobs (recipe follows)	1 serving Three-Way Chicken Kabobs ½ cup (125 mL) cooked brown rice or whole-wheat pasta	1 Vegetables and Fruit 1 Grain Products 1 Meat and Alternatives ½ Oils and Fats
Evening Snack Veggie Barley Salad (recipe follows)	1 serving Veggie Barley Salad	¾ Vegetables and Fruit ½ Grain Products 1 Oils and Fats
Total Servings:		6 ½ Vegetables and Fruit 6 ½ Grain Products 2 ¼ Meat and Alternatives 3 Milk and Alternatives 4 ½ Oils and Fats

Good To Know

Nutrition facts of the day	Adjusting today's menu
Calories: 1676 Fat: 49 g Saturated fat: 12 g Carbohydrate: 218 g Fibre: 26 g Protein: 100 g	*To cut about 200 calories* · Reduce milk to ½ cup (125 mL) at breakfast (saves 50 kcal) · Add only 1 tsp (5 mL) canola oil to the salad pita at lunch (saves 40 kcal) · Cut serving size of Veggie Barley Salad evening snack in half (saves 110 kcal) *To add about 200 calories* · Use 2 oz (55 g) beef tenderloin to make the salad pita (adds 125 kcal) · Drink ½ cup (125 mL) orange juice with lunch (adds 55 kcal) · Drink ½ cup (125 mL) of 1% milk with dinner (adds 50 kcal) and increase brown rice to ¾ cup (175 mL) (adds 50 kcal)

Garden Fresh Frittata

Serves 4 - Serving Size: 1 wedge or ¼ of the frittata

Ingredients:

1 Tbsp	canola oil	15 mL
1 cup	diced onions	250 mL
1 cup	thinly sliced yellow squash	250 mL
6	large eggs	6
¼ cup	1% milk	60 mL
2 Tbsp	chopped fresh basil	30 mL
¼ tsp	salt	1 mL
¼ tsp	black pepper, or to taste	1 mL
1 cup	packed baby spinach	250 mL
1 cup	grape tomatoes, quartered	250 mL
¼ tsp	salt	1 mL
¼ cup	chopped fresh basil, divided	60 mL
1 ½ oz	feta cheese, crumbled	45 g

Directions:

1. Heat the canola oil in a medium nonstick skillet over medium heat. Cook the onions for 3 minutes or until translucent; add the squash and cook for 4 minutes or until just tender, stirring frequently.

2. In a small bowl, whisk together the eggs, milk, 2 Tbsp (30 mL) of the basil, ¼ tsp (1 mL) of the salt and the black pepper and set aside.

3. Reduce the heat to medium-low. Sprinkle the spinach evenly over the squash mixture, then pour the egg mixture evenly over all. Sprinkle evenly with the tomatoes and remaining ¼ tsp (1 mL) salt.

4. Cover and cook for 12 minutes or until eggs are just set. Remove from heat.

5. Sprinkle evenly with the remaining basil and cheese. Let stand, uncovered, for 5 minutes to absorb flavours and firm slightly. Cut into wedges to serve.

About This Recipe: Start your day off right with a frittata that's prepared on the stovetop! No oven-proof skillet required for this delicious breakfast.

Per Serving: 201 kcal, 12 g fat, 4 g saturated fat, 9 g carbohydrate, 2 g fibre, 14 g protein.

Quick Tip: This makes a great Meatless Monday dinner, too! Just add a small tossed salad and a dinner roll.

Chef's Tip: Substitute the feta with ¼ cup (60 mL) shredded mozzarella plus 1½ Tbsp (25 mL) grated Parmesan cheese. Substitute peppers or sweet potatoes for the squash.

Cracker Melts
Serves 2 - Serving Size: 5 scoops

Ingredients:

10	scoop-shaped multigrain tortilla chips	10
2	Roma tomatoes, chopped	2
1 ½ oz	low-fat shredded mozzarella cheese	40 g

Directions:

1. Divide tomatoes and cheese evenly and place into scoops.

2. Microwave until cheese is melted (about 30 seconds).

Variations: Try scoops with prepared or homemade low-sodium tomato salsa as shown in the photo. Or use the same topping on Melba toast or thin slices of whole-wheat baguette.

About This Recipe: Enjoy this crunchy snack to get a serving of grains, dairy, and vegetables in one!
Per Serving: 128 kcal, 5 g fat, 1 g saturated fat, 15 g carbohydrate, 2 g fibre, 7 g protein.

Healthy Tip: Try adding diced red peppers, green onions, jalapenos and olives for extra flavour and an additional source of veggies!

Purple Dinosaur
Serves 2 - Serving Size: 1 ⅛ cup (280 mL)

Ingredients:

¼ cup	frozen 100% grape juice concentrate	60 mL
1 cup	low-fat vanilla yogurt	250 mL
1 cup	1% milk	250 mL

Directions:

1. Put the ingredients into a blender container. Blend until smooth (about 10 seconds).

2. Pour into two glasses and serve immediately. Enjoy!

 About This Recipe: This smoothie is a great source of calcium for kids (and adults) who avoid drinking milk!

Per Serving: 205 kcal, 3 g fat, 2 g saturated fat, 35 g carbohydrate, 0 fibre, 10 g protein.

 Healthy Tip: This simple recipe provides 1 ½ servings Milk & Alternatives according to *Eating Well with Canada's Food Guide*. It's a great way to boost calcium intake and to keep your bones healthy! For added fibre and flavour, add 1 cup (250 mL) of berries.

Three-Way Chicken Kabobs

Serves 4 - Serving Size: 1 kabob and 1 Tbsp (15 mL) sauce

Ingredients:

Italian:

1 lb	boneless chicken breast, cut into 16 pieces	450 g
1	medium zucchini, halved lengthwise and cut into 8 pieces each	1
1	medium red bell pepper, seeded and cut into 16 pieces	1
2 Tbsp	canola oil	30 mL
2 Tbsp	cider vinegar	30 mL
1	medium garlic clove, minced	1
¼ tsp	dried pepper flakes, optional	1 mL
½ tsp	salt	2 mL
2 Tbsp	chopped fresh oregano leaves	30 mL

Mexican:

1 lb	boneless chicken breast, cut into 16 pieces	450 g
16	cherry tomatoes	16
1	medium green bell pepper, seeded and cut into 16 pieces	1
2 Tbsp	canola oil	30 mL
2 Tbsp	lemon juice	30 mL
1 tsp	ground cumin	5 mL
¼ tsp	cayenne (optional)	1 mL
½ tsp	salt	2 mL
2 Tbsp	finely chopped fresh cilantro leaves	30 mL

Thai:

1 lb	boneless chicken breast, cut into 16 pieces	450 g
16	whole mushrooms	16
4	green onions, ends trimmed and cut into 1-inch (2.5 cm) pieces	4
2 Tbsp	canola oil	30 mL
2 Tbsp	fresh lime juice	30 mL
2 tsp	grated ginger	10 mL
1 tsp	hot pepper sauce (optional)	5 mL
½ tsp	salt	2 mL
1 Tbsp	finely chopped fresh basil leaves	15 mL
1 Tbsp	finely chopped fresh cilantro leaves	15 mL

Directions:

1. Preheat grill to medium-high heat. Coat grill rack with canola-based cooking spray.

2. Thread the chicken and vegetables onto 4 skewers. Grill, uncovered 8-10 minutes or until the chicken is cooked through, turning occasionally. To be safe, the chicken should be at an internal temperature of 170°F (77°C).

3. Meanwhile, whisk together the remaining ingredients, except the fresh herbs, in a small bowl. Place skewers on dinner plates, and spoon equal amounts of the mixture over each serving and sprinkle evenly with the fresh herbs.

 About This Recipe: These chicken skewers are a great way to impress guests at a dinner party – but they're also easy to pack for lunch! Soak bamboo skewers in water for 30 minutes prior to threading chicken. This will prevent the skewers from burning when grilling the kabobs.

Per Serving: 205 kcal, 9 g fat, 2 g saturated fat, 4 g carbohydrate, 1 g fibre, 27 g protein.

Veggie Barley Salad

Serves 6 - Serving Size: Approximately 1 cup (250 mL)

Ingredients:

1 ¼ cups	reduced-sodium chicken broth or vegetable broth	300 mL
1 cup	quick-cooking barley	250 mL
1	medium tomato, seeded and chopped	1
1	small zucchini, halved and thinly sliced	1
1	small sweet yellow pepper, seeded and chopped	1
2 Tbsp	minced fresh parsley	30 mL

Dressing:

3 Tbsp	canola oil	45 mL
2 Tbsp	apple cider vinegar or balsamic vinegar	30 mL
1 Tbsp	water	15 mL
1 Tbsp	lemon juice	15 mL
1 Tbsp	minced fresh basil	15 mL
½ tsp	salt	2 mL
¼ tsp	pepper	1 mL
¼ cup	slivered almonds, toasted	60 mL

Directions:

1. In a small saucepan, bring the broth and barley to a boil. Reduce heat; cover and simmer for 10-12 minutes or until barley is tender. Remove from the heat; let stand for 5 minutes then refrigerate to chill.

2. In a large bowl combine the tomato, zucchini, yellow pepper and parsley. Stir in barley.

3. In a small bowl whisk the oil vinegar, water, lemon juice, basil, salt and pepper. Pour over barley mixture; toss to coat. Cover and refrigerate for at least 3 hours.

4. Just before serving, stir in almonds.

About This Recipe: This salad packs a punch! Fresh parsley and basil give barley and veggies a ton of flavour.

Per Serving: 223 kcal, 10 g fat, 0.9 g saturated fat, 28 g carbohydrate, 7 g fibre, 6 g protein.

About Physical Activity

Healthy eating goes great with physical activity! Health Canada recommends that adults get 30 minutes of moderate to vigorous physical activity most days of the week. Children should get at least twice that amount.

Physical activity benefits include aerobic fitness, muscle and bone strength, better overall metabolism and improved mental health and relief from stress. Physical activity lowers risks associated with developing type 2 diabetes, cardiovascular disease and certain cancers. In children, being physically active helps develop healthy bones, improves coordination and runs off excess energy for better concentration in school.

New research also suggests that sedentary behaviours contribute to risks of future poor health. Limit time spent watching television, playing video or computer games, sitting or doing other passive activities. Try to use active transportation like bicycling or walking whenever possible.

What is moderate to vigorous physical activity?
Moderate – sufficient to increase your heart and breathing rates - brisk walking, biking at a moderate pace, golf, gardening and playground activities.

Vigorous – think "aerobic" – enough to make it hard to carry on a conversation during the activity – jogging and running, biking at a faster pace, tennis, many team sports. Swimming at a relatively slow pace is considered "moderate" activity even if you can't talk while doing it.

What about aerobic versus resistance exercise?
Aerobic exercises are activities that increase your heart and breathing rates – usually something that involves locomotion through water, across the ground, on a bike or a treadmill. Resistance exercises are activities designed to increase the size of your muscles and generally involve pushing or pulling against a resistance, like working with hand-weights, pulling on elastic bands or paddling a canoe or kayak. Some household activities that qualify as resistance exercise include digging in the garden, stacking firewood and so on.

Activities that help to maintain flexibility should also be included for overall good health.

Sources of Week 3 Recipes – From the PANDA Nutrition Team

Mixed Grain and Lentil Pilaf *(developed by Nancy Hughes)*
Coconutty Rhubarb Crisp
Tuna Open-Faced Sandwich with Bacon *(developed by Nancy Hughes)*
Sweet Spiced Carrot Muffins *(developed by Nancy Hughes)*
Berry Citrus Brown Betty *(developed by Nancy Hughes)*
Three-Way Chicken Kabobs *(developed by Nancy Hughes)*
Cracker Melts *(developed by Nancy Hughes)*
Garden Fresh Frittata *(developed by Nancy Hughes)*
Crispy Pear and Cabbage Salad *(developed by Nancy Hughes)*
Roasted Veggie, Fresh Veggie Salsa *(developed by Nancy Hughes)*
Stovetop Shepherd's Pie *(developed by Nancy Hughes)*
Roasted Vegetables

Used with Permission

Progessive Foods Inc: Veggie Barley Salad
Dairy Farmers of Canada: Chicken Noodle Bowl
Canada Beef: Marinated Steak with Melted Onions
CanolaInfo.org: Orange-Glazed Salmon and Sauteed Spinach, Cucumber and Black Bean Salsa Salad, Healthy Borscht Soup, Chicken with Lime, Garlic and Cashews, Warm Salmon Pasta Salad
Taste of Home: Mediterranean Chicken Stir-Fry, Breakfast Banana Raisin Wraps, Chili Popcorn, Garlic-Pepper Tenderloin Steak
Canadian Living Magazine: Vegetarian Cabbage Rolls
Alberta Milk: Banana and Cranberry Bread Pudding, Purple Dinosaur, Fruity Breakfast Oats

For more recipes visit: www.pureprairie.ca

Average Intakes of Week 3:

By Food Group:	By Nutrient Profile:
8 Vegetables and Fruit 7 Grains 3 Meat and Alternatives 3 Milk and Alternatives	1916 kcal total energy 49 g fat (26 % of total energy) 12 g saturated fat (7 % of total energy) 218 g carbohydrate (52 % of total energy) 26 g fibre 100 g protein (22% of total energy)

Grocery List Week 4

Food Group	Food Item	
Vegetables & Fruit	Apples*†	Peas, snap, fresh *†
	Avocados	Peppers, poblano / jalapeno†
	Basil, fresh*†	Peppers*, sweet, green / red / yellow*†
	Blueberries or Saskatoons*, fresh / frozen†	Pineapple
	Berries, mixed, fresh or frozen	Pumpkin, canned
	Broccoli*	Potatoes*†
	Carrots*†	Romaine lettuce / Salad greens*†
	Celery*	Rosemary, fresh*
	Cilantro, fresh*†	Shallots*
	Coleslaw mix	Spinach*†
	Cranberry sauce	Strawberries*, fresh or frozen†
	Cucumber*†	Tomatoes*, Roma / grape†
	Garlic*†	Zucchini*†
	Gingerroot†	
	Green beans*	
	Green Onion*†	
	Horseradish, fresh	
	Kale*	
	Lemons†	
	Limes†	
	Mint, fresh*†	
	Mushrooms*†	
	Onions*, yellow / red†	
	Oranges, mandarin / juice†	
	Parsley, fresh*†	
	Parsnip*†	
Grain Products	Bread, whole-wheat*†	
	Bread, pumpernickel	
	English muffin, whole-wheat*†	
	Sunny Boy Hot Cereal*	
	Tortillas, whole-wheat / corn†	
	Crackers, whole wheat*	
Milk & Alternatives	Buttermilk, low-fat*	
	Cheddar cheese, low-fat*†	
	Cottage cheese, low-fat	
	Milk, 1% M.F. or skim*†	
	Mozzarella and cheddar blend, shredded*†	
	Sour cream, low-fat	
	Yogurt, low-fat, Greek-style*†	
	Yogurt, low-fat, vanilla / fruit*†	
Meat & Alternatives	Canadian Bacon	
	Chicken breast	
	Eggs*†	
	Fish Fillets (walleye*, halibut, cod, trout*)	
	Ground beef* or turkey*	
	Hummus* (or use recipe provided in week 1)	
	Sirloin beef steak*†	
	Turkey breast*	

Prairie-produced foods.
†*Foods also listed in week 3*

Week 4, Day 1

Meal	Ingredients per Serving	Canada's Food Guide Servings
Breakfast Sunny Boy Hot Cereal with Milk and Fruit	¼ cup (40 g) (dry) Sunny Boy hot cereal, prepared according to directions 1 cup (250 mL) 1% milk 1 apple or ½ cup (125 mL) fruit of choice 1 cup (250 mL) coffee / tea 2 Tbsp (30 mL) 1% milk (optional) 1 tsp (5 mL) granulated sugar (optional)	1 Vegetables and Fruit 1 Grain Products 1 Milk and Alternatives
Morning Snack Lemon Berry Mini Pancakes (recipe follows)	1 serving Lemon Berry Mini Pancakes	½ Grain Products 1 Milk and Alternatives
Lunch Lentil Burritos (recipe follows)	1 serving Lentil Burritos	1 Vegetables and Fruit 2 Grain Products ¼ Meat and Alternatives ¼ Oils and Fats
Afternoon Snack Peanut Butter Sandwich	2 slices whole-wheat bread 2 Tbsp (30 mL) peanut butter ½ cup (125 mL) 1% milk	2 Grain Products 1 Meat and Alternatives ½ Milk and Alternatives
Dinner Chicken Tikka Masala (recipe follows)	1 serving Chicken Tikka Masala	3 Vegetables and Fruit 1 Grain Products 1 ½ Meat and Alternatives ½ Milk and Alternatives 1 Oils and Fats
Evening Snack Mixed Fruits with Roasted Almonds	½ cup (125 mL) cantaloupe, cubed ½ cup (125 mL) fresh strawberries, halved 1 Tbsp (15 mL) roasted almonds	2 Vegetables and Fruit ¼ Meat and Alternatives
Total Servings:		7 Vegetables and Fruit 6 ½ Grain Products 3 Meat and Alternatives 3 Milk and Alternatives 1 ¼ Oils and Fats

Good To Know

Nutrition facts of the day	Adjusting today's menu
Calories: 1972 Fat: 63 g Saturated fat: 11 g Carbohydrate: 267 g Fibre: 48 g Protein: 99 g	*To cut about 200 calories* · Have ½ cup (125 mL) 1% milk at breakfast (saves 50 kcal) · Have one 1 slice of toast and peanut butter at afternoon snack (saves 130 kcal) *To add about 200 calories* · Increase milk to 1 cup (250 mL) at afternoon snack (adds 50 kcal) · Add 1 tsp (5 mL) canola oil to green beans at dinner (adds 40 kcal) · Add 2 Tbsp (30 mL) sunflower seeds to evening snack (adds 90 kcal)

Lemon Berry Mini Pancakes

Serves 4 - Serving Size: 4 pancakes

Ingredients:

Pancakes:

½ cup	all-purpose flour	125 mL
½ cup	whole-wheat flour	125 mL
1 Tbsp	granulated sugar	15 mL
1 tsp	baking powder	5 mL
¼ tsp	baking soda	1 mL
¼ tsp	salt	1 mL
¾ cup	1% milk	175 mL
2 tsp	grated lemon zest	10 mL
2 Tbsp	fresh lemon juice	30 mL
1 Tbsp	canola oil	15 mL
1	large egg	1
1 Tbsp	canola oil	15 mL

Topping:

1 cup	Saskatoon berries or blueberries*	250 mL
1 cup	raspberries*	250 mL
1 Tbsp	granulated sugar	15 mL
1 tsp	vanilla extract	5 mL
½ cup	fat-free plain Greek yogurt	125 mL

*If using frozen berries, make sure that they are thawed before mixing the topping. Place in microwave for approximately 1 minute to warm the berries up quickly.

Directions:

1. Whisk the flours, 1 Tbsp (15 mL) sugar, baking powder, baking soda and salt in a large bowl. Whisk together the milk, lemon zest, lemon juice, 1 tablespoon of the canola oil and the egg in a medium bowl. Add to flour mixture, stirring just until moist. Let stand for 15 minutes.

2. Preheat oven to 200°F (95°C) to keep the pancakes warm until they are ready to be served. Combine the topping ingredients (except yogurt) in a medium bowl and set aside.

3. Working in 3 batches, heat 1 Tbsp (15 mL) of canola oil in a large non-stick skillet over medium heat. Tilt skillet to lightly coat bottom of pan. Spoon approximately 2 Tbsp (30 mL) of batter onto skillet (for each pancake). Cook for 2 minutes, or until bubbles form and burst, and edges of pancakes appear cooked. Flip and cook for 2 minutes longer, or until slightly puffed and golden on bottom. Place on an oven-safe serving platter and place in oven to keep warm while the remaining pancakes are cooked.

4. Serve with topping and yogurt.

> **⚠ About This Recipe:** The zesty lemon in these pancakes contrasts with the sweetness of the berries and the tartness of the yogurt.
>
> *Per Serving: 288 kcal, 9 g fat, 1 g saturated fat, 43 g carbohydrate, 5 g fibre, 10 g protein.*

Lentil Burritos
Serves 4 - Serving Size: 1 burrito

Ingredients:

¾ cup	split red lentils	175 mL
1 ½ cups	water	375 mL
1 tsp	canola oil	5 mL
½	medium onion, diced	½
½ cup	green pepper, diced	125 mL
1	large garlic cloves, minced	1
¾ tsp	chili powder	3 mL
¼ tsp	ground cumin	1 mL
½ cup	water	125 mL
3 Tbsp	tomato paste	45 mL
4	6-inch (15 cm) whole grain tortillas	4
4 Tbsp	fat-free sour cream, divided	60 mL
4 Tbsp	salsa, divided	60 mL
4 Tbsp	shredded low-fat cheddar cheese	60 mL

Directions:

1. Rinse and drain lentils. In saucepan, bring lentils to a boil, cover and simmer for 20 minutes. Slightly undercook. Drain if necessary.

2. In sauté pan, sauté onion, green pepper and garlic in canola oil, but do not brown. Add chili powder, cumin, cooked lentils, water and tomato paste. Stir for 2 minutes until the mixture starts to thicken. Cover and cook for another 5 minutes.

3. Lay tortilla flat and place ½ cup (125 mL) of lentil mix down in center and roll up. Top each burrito with 1 Tbsp (15 mL) each of sour cream, salsa and cheese.

 About This Recipe: Lentils make these vegetarian burritos filling and satisfying. Throw some jalapenos in for a spicy kick.

Per Serving: 270 kcal, 5 g fat, 0.6 g saturated fat, 41 g carbohydrate, 15 g fibre, 16 g protein.

 Healthy Tip: Lentils have one of the highest levels of protein among legumes and nuts. In combination with whole grain tortilla, this nutritious recipe is a source of complete protein and is also rich in dietary fibre. For variations, use green, black or other lentils.

Chicken Tikka Masala

Serves 4 - Serving Size: 1 ¼ cups (310 mL)

Ingredients:

⅔ cup	dry brown rice	150 mL
1 ¼ cup	water	310 mL
1 Tbsp	canola oil	15 mL
12 oz	boneless, skinless chicken breast, chopped	350 g
1 Tbsp	canola oil	15 mL
1 ½	cups diced onion	375 mL
1 ½ tsp	curry powder	7 mL
1 tsp	ground cumin	5 mL
¼ tsp	cayenne pepper	1 mL
1 can	14.5 oz (429 mL) low-salt canned stewed tomatoes	1 can
1 can	16 oz (500 g) chickpeas, drained and rinsed	1 can
1 tsp	granulated sugar	5 mL
½ cup	frozen green peas	125 mL
¼ cup	fresh cilantro, chopped	60 mL
2 tsp	fresh grated ginger	10 mL
½ tsp	salt	2 mL
½ cup	fat-free plain Greek yogurt	125 mL
1	medium lime, cut into 4 wedges	1
¼ cup	fresh cilantro, chopped	60 mL

Directions:

1. Cook brown rice in 1 ¼ cups (300 mL) of water in a pot over the stove. Bring rice and water to a boil uncovered, then place lid on pot and reduce heat to let rice simmer for approximately 20 minutes. After 20 minutes, turn heat off and let rice sit for another 10-15 minutes, or until cooked.

2. Heat 1 Tbsp (15 mL) canola oil in a large non-stick skillet over medium-high heat. Cook chicken for 3 minutes, or until lightly browned. Use a food thermometer to ensure that the chicken has reached an internal temperature of 170°F (77°C), or cook the chicken until no longer pink in the centre. Set chicken aside on a separate plate.

3. Heat remaining 1 Tbsp (15 mL) canola oil, cook the onions for 5 minutes or until they begin to brown. Add curry, cumin, and cayenne. Cook for 15 seconds or until fragrant, stirring constantly. Stir in the tomatoes, chickpeas, chicken, any accumulated juices and sugar. Reduce heat to medium-low, cover, and cook for 15 minutes or until onions are tender. Remove from heat.

4. Stir in the peas, ¼ cup (60 mL) of the cilantro, ginger, and salt. Serve over rice, topped with Greek yogurt, remaining cilantro and lime wedges.

About This Recipe: This mild curry dish rivals traditional Indian dishes. The Greek yogurt adds a refreshing contrast to the flavour of the onions and the curry.

Per Serving: 474 kcal, 11 g fat, 2 g saturated fat, 62 g carbohydrate, 10 g fibre, 32 g protein.

About Pulses (including Chickpeas)

Packed with nutrients that help heart health, including fibre, folate, and potassium, pulses (including chickpeas) are also low in fat and cholesterol-free. In addition to being a healthful part of the diet of people with high cholesterol or diabetes, pulses are suitable for vegetarian, vegan and gluten-free diets as well.

In Canada, chickpeas are mainly grown in the southern, arid regions of Alberta and Saskatchewan.

In cooking, try adding drained, rinsed canned chickpeas to rice dishes, soups, chili or pasta. One ¾ cup (175 mL) serving of cooked chickpeas is an excellent source of protein, fibre and folate. It also contains a significant amount of calcium and only 1 g fat.

There are an amazing variety of pulses. Try some today!

Week 4, Day 2

Meal	Ingredients per Serving	Canada's Food Guide Servings
Breakfast Apricot-Ginger Granola (recipe follows)	1 serving Apricot-Ginger Granola ½ cup (125 mL) 1% milk 1 cup (250 mL) coffee / tea 2 Tbsp (30 mL) 1% milk (optional) 1 tsp (5 mL) granulated sugar (optional)	½ Vegetables and Fruit 2 Grain Products ½ Meat and Alternatives ½ Milk and Alternatives
Morning Snack Celery Sticks and Hummus (see week 1)	½ cup (125 mL) celery sticks ¼ cup (60 mL) hummus	1 Vegetables and Fruit ½ Meat and Alternatives
Lunch Mushroom Barley Soup with Romaine Pecan Salad (recipe follows)	1 serving Mushroom Barley Soup 1 whole-wheat dinner roll 1 cup (250 mL) Romaine lettuce ¼ cup (60 mL) cucumber 1 Tbsp (15 mL) pecan halves 1 Tbsp (15 mL) fat-free Italian dressing	3 Vegetables and Fruit 1 ¼ Grain Products ¼ Meat and Alternatives 1 Oils and Fats
Afternoon Snack Trail Mix	2 Tbsp (30 mL) mixed nuts / seeds of choice ¼ cup (60 mL) dried mixed fruits of choice	1 Vegetables and Fruit ½ Meat and Alternatives
Dinner Pasta Florentine Bake (recipe follows)	1 serving Pasta Florentine Bake 1 whole-wheat dinner roll ½ cup (125 mL) carrot sticks ½ cup (125 mL) broccoli florets	2 ½ Vegetables and Fruit 2 Grain Products ½ Meat and Alternatives ½ Milk and Alternatives
Evening Snack Pumpkin Flan (recipe follows)	1 serving Pumpkin Flan ¾ cup (175 mL) 1% milk	¼ Vegetables and Fruit ¼ Meat and Alternatives 1 Milk and Alternatives 1 Oils and Fats
Total Servings:		8 Vegetables and Fruit 5 ¼ Grain Products 2 ½ Meat and Alternatives 2 Milk and Alternatives 2 Oils and Fats

Good To Know

Nutrition facts of the day	Adjusting today's menu
Calories: 1816 Fat: 58 g Saturated fat: 12 g Carbohydrate: 228 g Fibre: 42 g Protein: 115 g	*To cut about 200 calories* · Have 2 Tbsp (30 mL) low-fat ranch dressing with celery sticks at morning snack instead of hummus (saves 40 kcal) · Skip the dinner roll at dinner (saves 75 kcal) · Skip the cottage cheese to prepare the pasta at dinner (saves 80 kcal) *To add about 200 calories* · At morning snack, have 2 Tbsp (30 mL) peanut butter instead of hummus (adds 80 kcal) and drink ½ cup (125 mL) orange juice (adds 55 kcal) · Add a slice of whole-wheat toast to evening snack (adds 70 kcal)

Apricot-Ginger Granola

Serves 18 - Serving Size: ⅓ cup (75 mL)

Ingredients:

2 cups	high fibre cereal, e.g. All Bran Buds	500 mL
2 cups	rolled oats	500 mL
1 cup	pecans or walnuts, chopped	250 mL
½ cup	sunflower seeds	125 mL
⅓ cup	packed brown sugar	75 mL
3 Tbsp	canola oil	45 mL
1 tsp	ground cinnamon	5 mL
½ tsp	ground nutmeg	2 mL
½ tsp	salt	2 mL
12	dried apricot halves, chopped	12
1 Tbsp	fresh grated ginger	15 mL

Directions:

1. Preheat oven to 300°F (150°C).

2. In a large bowl, combine the cereal, oats, pecans, sunflower seeds, sugar, canola oil, cinnamon, nutmeg, and salt. Place on a baking sheet, and bake for 12 minutes. Remove from oven, stir, and bake for an additional 5 minutes, or until the granola begins to lightly brown. Remove from oven.

3. Stir in remaining ingredients. Serve warm or cooled.

 About This Recipe: Enjoy this granola plain, or serve topped with fresh fruit and yogurt. Change up the nuts, seeds, and dried fruit and you'll have a different flavour every time!

Per Serving: 164 kcal, 9 g fat, 0.9 g saturated fat, 21 g carbohydrate, 6 g fibre, 3 g protein.

 Healthy Tip: Granola can be high in fat and sugar. Make sure you read labels and pick a brand that is low in fat and sugar or use this recipe to make your own without a lot of added sugars.

Mushroom Barley Soup
Serves 6 - Serving Size: Approximately 2 cups (500 mL)

Ingredients:

5 ½ cups	low-sodium vegetable broth	1.375 L
1 cup	quick-cooking barley	250 mL
½ cup	chopped green onion	125 mL
2 cloves	garlic, minced	2 cloves
1	basil leaf	1
½ tsp	Worcestershire sauce	2 mL
⅛ tsp	pepper	0.5 mL
2 cups	sliced fresh assorted mushrooms	500 mL
¾ cup	shredded carrot	175 mL
3 Tbsp	snipped fresh parsley	45 mL
½ cup	chopped celery	125 mL

Directions:

1. In a large saucepan, bring vegetable broth to boiling. Stir in onion, garlic, basil, Worcestershire sauce and pepper. Cover and simmer for about 10 minutes.

2. Stir in mushrooms, carrot and celery. Add quick-cooking barley, cover and let simmer for about 20 minutes. Sprinkle with parsley.

About This Recipe: Fresh veggies make this healthy soup stand out. Barley is grown and processed in Canada's prairie provinces! All of the vegetables in this soup are produced locally in season, and mushrooms are locally available all year round.

Per Serving: 190 kcal, 1 g fat, 0.3 g saturated fat, 37 g carbohydrate, 9 g fibre, 7 g protein.

Quick Tip: Quick-cooking barley reduces the cooking time of any barley dish, when compared to pot or pearl barley – and it still has the nutritional benefits!

Pasta Florentine Bake
Serves 6 - Serving Size: Approximately 1 ½ cups (375 mL)

Ingredients:

	canola oil cooking spray	
1 ½ cups	small shell pasta, about 300 g (whole-wheat)	375 mL
½ can	19 oz (540 mL) Italian seasoned stewed tomatoes	½ can
½ can	28 oz (796 mL) crushed / ground tomatoes	½ can
1 ½ cups	Big Batch Ground Beef *	375 mL
1 ½ cups	chopped kale	375 mL
½ tsp	dried oregano	2 mL
½ tsp	dried basil	2 mL
¼ tsp	salt	1 mL
½ cup	low-fat cottage cheese	125 mL
½ cup	shredded mozzarella and Parmesan cheese blend	125 mL

Directions:

1. Cook pasta according to package directions; drain and set aside.

2. Meanwhile, heat stewed tomatoes in Dutch oven, over medium heat, breaking up with wooden spoon. Stir in crushed tomatoes, Big Batch Beef, kale, oregano, basil and salt; bring to a simmer and heat through. Stir in cottage cheese.

3. Stir in reserved cooked pasta. Transfer mixture to a lightly oiled 9 x 13 inch (22 x 33 cm) casserole dish; top with cheese and bake in 350°F (180°C) oven until bubbly, 15-20 minutes.

*Big Batch Ground Beef: Cook 4 lb (2 kg) lean or extra-lean ground beef in Dutch oven over medium-high heat for 10-15 minutes, breaking into small chunks with back of spoon, until browned. Drain and return to pot. Add 4 each onion and cloves of garlic, minced, simmer for 15 minutes until vegetables are softened. Use a food thermometer to ensure that the beef has reached an internal temperature of 160°F (71°C). Drain and spread in a single layer on baking trays; freeze until meat is firm, about 1 hour. Loosen into chunks, scoop meal-sized portions into freezer bags. Freeze for up to 3 months.

 About This Recipe: Pasta and cheese - yes please! Chopped kale and tomatoes add extra flavour to this dish when combined with basil and oregano.

Per Serving: 637 kcal, 15 g fat, 6 g saturated fat, 55 g carbohydrate, 8 g fibre, 51 g protein.

 Healthy Tip: Beef is a source of monounsaturated fats, which are also found in canola and olive oils, avocados, and nuts such as almonds. Monounsaturated fats may help lower your risk of heart disease but be cautious of the number of calories in fats, so use in moderation.

Pumpkin Flan
Serves 8 - Serving Size: 1 flan

Ingredients:

	canola oil cooking spray	
3	eggs, omega-3-enriched (if available)	3
1 ¼ cup	pumpkin puree	300 mL
½ cup	maple syrup	125 mL
2 Tbsp	canola oil	30 mL
1 ½ tsp	pure vanilla extract	7 mL
¾ tsp	ground cinnamon	4 mL
¼ tsp	ground ginger	1 mL
¼ tsp	ground cloves	1 mL
¼ tsp	salt	1 mL
1 ½ cups	low-fat milk, heated until very hot but not boiling	375 mL
1 quart	boiling water for water bath ground nutmeg for garnish	1 L

Directions:

1. Preheat oven to 350°F (180°C). Adjust oven rack to centre position. Coat eight 6 oz custard cups or ramekins with canola oil cooking spray and set them in 13 x 9 inch (33 x 22 cm) baking pan.

2. In large bowl, beat eggs slightly; add pumpkin purée, maple syrup, canola oil, vanilla, spices and salt. Beat with mixer until blended thoroughly. Stir in hot milk until blended. There will be about 4 cups (1 L) of liquid. Pour ½ cup (125 mL) flan mixture into each prepared ramekin.

3. Carefully pour boiling water into baking pan around ramekins. Water should come up to level of custard inside ramekins.

4. Bake 40-45 minutes or until set around the edges but still a little loose in centre. When centre of flan is just set, it will jiggle a little when shaken. Remove from oven and immediately remove ramekins from water bath; cool on wire rack until flan reaches room temperature. Cover with plastic wrap and refrigerate.

5. Serve cold garnish with ground nutmeg just prior to serving. This dessert can be made up to a maximum of 3 days in advance. Keep refrigerated until serving.

 About This Recipe: These flans aren't just for holiday dinners, they can be enjoyed any time of the year with the perfect blend of sweet spices. Pumpkin is an excellent source of vitamin A.

Per Serving: 144 kcal, 6 g fat, 1 g saturated fat, 19 g carbohydrate, 2 g fibre, 5 g protein.

 Quick Tip: Use leftover pumpkin purée in a smoothie with yogurt, milk, sweet spices (cinnamon, ginger, cloves) and a drizzle of agave nectar, honey or maple syrup.

Head to Head: How the Nutrients Stack Up

Meat, Poultry, Fish: Eating Well with Canada's Food Guide recommends 2-3 Meat and Alternatives servings each day for adults. Choose lean cuts, trim fat (and skin) and cook without added fat.

	Sirloin steak, trimmed of visible fat - 3 oz (75 g) - broiled	*Chicken, light meat, skinless - 3 oz (75 g) - roasted*	*Salmon - 3 oz (75 g) - baked or broiled*
Energy (kcal)	129	115	134
Protein (g)	22	20	18
Carbohydrate (g)	0	0	0
Total Fat (g)	3.9	3.1	6.2
Saturated fat (g)	1.7	0.8	1.5
Monounsaturated fat (g)	1.9	1.1	2.7
Omega-3 fat (g)	0.02	0.05	1.5

Week 4, Day 3

Meal	Ingredients per Serving	Canada's Food Guide Servings
Breakfast Hard Boiled Egg and Toast	2 eggs 2 slices whole-wheat bread 2 tsp (10 mL) non-hydrogenated margarine ½ cup (125 mL) canned peaches in water 1 cup (250 mL) coffee / tea 2 Tbsp (30 mL) 1% milk (optional) 1 tsp (5 mL) sugar (optional)	1 Vegetables and Fruit 2 Grain Products 1 Meat and Alternatives 2 Oils and Fats
Morning Snack Apple with Cheese	1 apple ¾ oz (22 g) low-fat cheddar cheese	1 Vegetables and Fruit ½ Milk and Alternatives
Lunch Cumin Corn Chowder with Pita Bread (recipe follows)	1 serving Cumin Corn Chowder 1 whole-wheat pita bread	3 Vegetables and Fruit 2 Grain Products ½ Milk and Alternatives
Afternoon Snack Snack Spinach Salad	2 Tbsp (30 mL) roasted almonds ¼ cup (60 mL) mandarin orange pieces 1 cup (250 mL) fresh spinach	1 ½ Vegetables and Fruit ½ Meat and Alternatives
Dinner Beef Sirloin with Fresh Horseradish-Mint Relish (recipe follows)	1 serving Beef Sirloin with Fresh Horseradish-Mint Relish 1 whole-wheat dinner roll ½ cup (125 mL) baby potatoes ½ cup (125 mL) green beans, steamed 1 cup (250 mL) 1% milk	2 Vegetables and Fruit 1 Grain Products 1 Meat and Alternatives 1 Milk and Alternatives ½ Oils and Fats
Evening Snack Peppermint Chocolate Chunk Cookies with Milk (recipe follows)	1 Peppermint Chocolate Chunk Cookie ½ cup (125 mL) 1% milk	1 Grain Products ½ Milk and Alternatives
Total Servings:		8 ½ Vegetables and Fruit 6 Grain Products 3 Meat and Alternatives 2 ½ Milk and Alternatives 2 ½ Oils and Fats

Good To Know

Nutrition facts of the day	Adjusting today's menu
Calories: 1839 Fat: 63 g Saturated fat: 13 g Carbohydrate: 240 g Fibre: 36 g Protein: 91 g	*To cut about 200 calories* · At breakfast, have one egg instead of two (saves 70 kcal) and skip margarine (saves 70 kcal) · Reduce milk to ½ cup (125 mL) at dinner (saves 50 kcal) *To add about 200 calories* · Have 1 All-Bran Bar with morning snack (adds 130 kcal) · Use a whole mandarin orange, about ½ cup (125 mL) to make the afternoon snack salad and add in 1 tsp (5 mL) canola oil (adds 65 kcal)

Cumin Corn Chowder

Serves 4 - Serving Size: 1 cup (250 mL)

Ingredients:

1 Tbsp	canola oil	15 mL
1 ½ cups	chopped red bell pepper	375 mL
1 ½ cups	small cauliflower florets	375 mL
1 ½ cups	frozen corn kernels	375 mL
1 cup	chopped green onions	250 mL
2 oz	reduced fat cream cheese, cut into small pieces	60 g
2 cups	skim milk	500 mL
1 tsp	ground cumin	5 mL
½ tsp	salt	2 mL
½ tsp	black pepper	2 mL
½ cup	chopped fresh cilantro or parsley	125 mL
1 oz	sharp cheddar cheese, shredded	28 g

Directions:

1. Heat the oil in a large saucepan over medium-high heat.

2. Add the bell pepper and cauliflower, cook for 8 minutes or until vegetables are tender, stirring occasionally.

3. Add the corn, green onions and cream cheese and stir until cheese melts. Add the milk and cook, covered, for 3 minutes or until heated through. (Do not bring to a boil.) Remove from heat.

4. Stir in the cumin, salt, black pepper and all but 2 Tbsp (30 mL) of the cilantro.

5. Cover and let stand for 10 minutes to absorb flavours. Spoon into bowls and top with the remaining cilantro and cheddar cheese.

 About This Recipe: This creamy soup is terrific on a chilly winter day.

Per Serving: 241 kcal, 10 g fat, 4 g saturated fat, 30 g carbohydrate, 4 g fibre, 11 g protein.

 Healthy Tip: Omit the salt in the soup and let the natural saltiness of the cheese along with the cilantro and cumin shine through.

Grilled Sirloin with Fresh Horseradish-Mint Relish

Serves 4 - Serving Size: 4 oz (115 g) steak

Ingredients:

½ tsp	coarsely ground black pepper	2 mL
¼ tsp	salt	1 mL
⅛ tsp	red pepper flakes	0.5 mL
1 lb	boneless beef sirloin steak, trimmed of fat	450 g
1 Tbsp	canola oil	15 mL

Relish:

½	medium poblano chili pepper, seeded and finely chopped	½
¼ cup	diced cucumber	60 mL
1 cup	diced tomato	250 mL
2 Tbsp	chopped fresh mint	30 mL
3 Tbsp	grated fresh horseradish	45 mL
1 ½ Tbsp	cider vinegar	22 mL
1 Tbsp	canola oil	15 mL
¼ tsp	salt	1 mL

Directions:

1. Preheat grill to medium-high heat.

2. Combine the ½ tsp (2 mL) black pepper, ¼ tsp (1mL) salt and pepper flakes in a small bowl. Brush both sides of the beef with 1 Tbsp (15 mL) of canola oil and sprinkle both sides of the beef with the pepper mixture.

3. Cook on grill for 4 minutes on each side or until desired doneness. Use a food thermometer to check internal temperatures: 145°F (65°C) for medium rare; 160°F (70°C) for medium; 170°F (75°C) for well done. Place on cutting board and let stand for 3 minutes before thinly slicing.

4. Meanwhile, combine relish ingredients in a medium bowl. Serve beef with relish and other green vegetables like asparagus.

About This Recipe: The high smoke point of canola oil makes it excellent for grilling Canadian-raised cuts of meat.
Per Serving: 265 kcal, 16 g fat, 4 g saturated fat, 5 g carbohydrate, 2 g fibre, 34 g protein.

Chef's Tip: You may substitute poblano with green bell pepper and ⅛ tsp (0.5 mL) dried pepper flakes. You may substitute fresh horseradish - use 1 Tbsp (15 mL) to start and adjust to taste.

Peppermint Chocolate Chunk Cookies

Serves 48 - Serving Size: 1 cookie

Ingredients:

2 cups	all-purpose flour	500 mL
1 cup	cake flour	250 mL
1 tsp	baking soda	5 mL
½ tsp	salt	2 mL
1 cup	canola oil	250 mL
1 ½ cups	packed brown sugar	375 mL
2	large eggs	2
2 tsp	pure vanilla extract	10 mL
½ tsp	peppermint extract	2 mL
12 oz	semi-sweet chocolate, cut into small chunks	350 g

Directions:

1. Preheat oven to 350°F (180°C). Line two baking sheets with parchment paper. Set aside.

2. In medium bowl, whisk together flours, baking soda and salt. Set aside.

3. In large bowl, whisk vigorously: canola oil, brown sugar, eggs, vanilla and peppermint extracts. Fold in flour mixture, mixing well. Fold in chocolate chunks.

4. Using an ice cream scoop, scoop dough onto prepared baking sheets. Press dough down firmly with palm of hand.

5. Bake until firm to touch, about 9-12 minutes. Cool on pan for 20 minutes; remove to rack to cool completely.

 About This Recipe: By using canola oil, saturated fat intake is minimized! Enjoy one of these indulgent cookies with a cup of herbal tea.

Per Serving: 137 kcal, 8 g fat, 2 g saturated fat, 17 g carbohydrate, 0.7 g fibre, 2 g protein.

 Chef's Tip: Cake flour has a different protein content than regular or bread flour, allowing for a different texture in baked goods.

Week 4, Day 4

Meal	Ingredients per Serving	Canada's Food Guide Servings
Breakfast Fruit Smoothie with English Muffin (see week 1)	1 serving Fruit Smoothie 1 whole-wheat English muffin 1 tsp (5 mL) non-hydrogenated margarine 1 tsp (5 mL) low-sugar strawberry jam 1 cup (250 mL) coffee / tea 2 Tbsp (30 mL) 1% milk (optional) 1 tsp (5 mL) sugar (optional)	2 Vegetables and Fruit 2 Grain Products 1 Milk and Alternatives 1 Oils and Fats
Morning Snack Breakfast-on-the-Go cookies (recipe follows)	1 Breakfast-on-the-Go cookie 1 cup (250 mL) 1% milk	1 Grain Products 1 Milk and Alternatives
Lunch Southwestern Turkey and Bean Salad with Garlic Toast and Milk (recipes follow)	1 serving Southwestern Turkey and Bean Salad 1 slice whole-wheat bread 1 tsp (5 mL) non-hydrogenated margarine 1 tsp (5 mL) grated Parmesan cheese 1 cup (250 mL) 1% milk	1 ½ Vegetables and Fruit 1 Grain Products 1 Meat and Alternatives 1 Milk and Alternatives 1 ½ Oils and Fats
Afternoon Snack Crackers and Easy Guacamole (recipe follows)	6 whole-wheat crackers (e.g. Triscuits) 1 serving Easy Guacamole	1 Vegetables and Fruit 1 Grain Products
Dinner Cumin Crusted Fish with Boiled Potatoes and Steamed Broccoli (recipe follows)	1 serving Cumin Crusted Fish ½ cup (125 mL) potatoes, steamed ½ cup (125 mL) broccoli, steamed 1 whole-wheat dinner roll	1 ½ Vegetables and Fruit 1 Grain Products 1 ½ Meat and Alternatives ½ Oils and Fats
Evening Snack Toast with Peanut Butter and Honey	1 slice whole-wheat bread 1 Tbsp (15 mL) peanut butter 1 tsp (5 mL) honey	1 Grain Products ½ Meat and Alternatives
Total Servings:		6 Vegetables and Fruit 7 Grain Products 3 Meat and Alternatives 3 Milk and Alternatives 3 Oils and Fats

Good To Know

Nutrition facts of the day	Adjusting today's menu
Calories:1854 Fat: 66 g Saturated fat: 13 g Carbohydrate: 247 g Fibre: 37 g Protein: 88 g	*To cut about 200 calories* · Have only half an English muffin at breakfast (saves 65 kcal) · Make the smoothie at breakfast by replacing ¼ cup (60 mL) low-fat yogurt with ¼ cup (60 mL) 1% milk (saves 25 kcal) · Reduce milk to ½ cup (125 mL) at morning snack (saves 50 kcal) · Have a slice of plain whole-wheat toast instead of garlic toast at lunch (saves 50 kcal) *To add about 200 calories* · Have 1 cup (250 mL) of potatoes and ½ cup (125 mL) steamed carrots at dinner (adds 95 kcal) · Drink a cup (250 mL) of 1% milk with evening snack (adds 100 kcal)

Breakfast-on-the-Go Cookies

Serves 24 - Serving Size: 1 cookie

Ingredients:

1 cup	brown sugar	250 mL
¼ cup	dry 7-grain hot cereal	60 mL
1 cup	rolled oats	250 mL
1 cup	all-purpose flour	250 mL
1 cup	whole-wheat flour	250 mL
1 ½ tsp	baking soda	7 mL
½ tsp	baking powder	2 mL
½ tsp	salt	2 mL
1 tsp	allspice	5 mL
¼ cup	canola oil	60 mL
¼ cup	applesauce	60 mL
3	egg whites	3
1 tsp	vanilla extract	5 mL
¼ cup	sunflower seeds	60 mL
⅓ cup	chopped dried cherries	75 mL

Directions:

1. Preheat oven to 350°F (180°C). Line cookie sheets with parchment paper.

2. In large bowl, stir together sugar, cereal, flours, baking soda, baking powder, salt and allspice. Make a well in the centre and pour in canola oil, applesauce, egg whites and vanilla.

3. Mix until well blended. Stir in sunflower seeds and cherries.

4. Roll cookies into golf ball-sized portions. Place cookies 2-inches (5 cm) apart onto prepared cookie sheets and flatten to ½-inch (1.3 cm) thickness with wet hands.

5. In preheated oven, bake for 8 minutes for chewy cookies. Remove from cookie sheets to cool on wire racks. Cookies may be frozen for up to one month.

 About This Recipe: These delicious fibre-rich cookies freeze well so enjoy a few fresh, and freeze the others in portion pack sealable bags for a busy on-the-go lifestyle.

Per Serving: 129 kcal, 4 g fat, 0.3 g saturated fat, 22 g carbohydrate, 2 g fibre, 3 g protein.

Southwestern Turkey
and Bean Salad with Garlic Toast
Serves 6 - Serving Size: Approximately 1 cup (250 mL)

Ingredients:

1 can	19 oz (540 mL) red kidney beans, rinsed and drained	1 can
1 can	12 oz (341 mL) corn kernels, drained	1 can
1	small carrot, chopped	1
½	red pepper, chopped	½
½ cup	sliced celery	125 mL
2	green onion, chopped	2
1 tsp	dried parsley	5 mL
1 cup	cooked turkey breast, diced	250 mL

Dressing:

¼ cup	red wine vinegar	60 mL
1 Tbsp	canola oil	15 mL
1	clove garlic, minced	1
¼ tsp	finely ground black pepper	1 mL
	hot sauce, to taste	

Directions:

1. In serving bowl, gently toss salad ingredients together.

2. In separate small bowl, whisk together dressing ingredients. Pour over salad and toss gently to combine. Chill for 30-60 minutes, stirring gently occasionally to blend flavours.

About This Recipe: This unique Mexican-inspired salad will satisfy your cravings on taco night! Add homemade corn tortilla chips for a well-balanced meal.

Per Serving: 148 kcal, 6 g fat, 3 g saturated fat, 23 g carbohydrate, 6 g fibre, 9 g protein.

Quick Tip: Line your bowl with a ½ serving of low-sodium tortilla chips for extra crunch.

Cook Once, Eat Twice or More: If you are roasting the turkey yourself, cook more so there's enough for tomorrow's lunch. Leftover kidney beans? Refrigerate in a sealed plastic container and use again later in the week. When buying canned corn kernels, choose the ones with no added salt to reduce sodium content of this recipe (or use frozen).

Garlic Toast

Serves 4 - Serving Size: 1 whole slice

Ingredients:

2 Tbsp	butter, softened or non-hydrogenated margarine	30 mL
4 slices	whole-wheat bread or baguette	4 slices
Dash	garlic salt	Dash
1 Tbsp	grated Parmesan cheese	15 mL

Directions:

1. Spread butter or margarine on one side of each slice of bread. Cut each slice in half; place plain side down on a baking sheet. Sprinkle with garlic salt and Parmesan cheese.

2. Broil 4-inches (10 cm) from the heat for 1-2 minutes or until lightly browned.

About This Recipe: The perfect toast for any Italian dish! It also pairs well with spaghetti squash as a pasta alternative, - so you get one serving of grains and one serving of vegetables from the squash!

Per Serving: 126 kcal, 7 g fat, 1 g saturated fat (using margarine), 12 g carbohydrate, 2 g fibre, 4 g protein.

Quick Tip: If garlic salt is not available, mix minced garlic, garlic powder, or garlic flakes with butter or margarine and spread on each bread slice. Finish with herbs that complement the rest of the meal, if desired.

Easy Guacamole
Serves 4 - Serving Size: Approximately ½ cup (125 mL)

Ingredients:

2	**ripe avocados, halved, pitted and peeled**	2
1	**Roma tomato, chopped**	1
½ cup	**green onion, chopped**	125 mL
1	**garlic clove, minced**	1
1 Tbsp	**low-fat yogurt**	15 mL
1 tsp	**lemon juice**	5 mL
½ tsp	**sesame oil (optional)**	2 mL
	salt and pepper to taste	

Directions:

1. Cut avocados into small cubes. In a large bowl, mash avocados with a potato masher to desired consistency.

2. Stir in tomato, green onion, garlic, yogurt, lemon juice and sesame oil. Divide into individual portions and serve.

 About This Recipe: Guacamole tastes great on everything! Try it with a broiled chicken breast or with tonight's dinner, Cumin Crusted Fish.

Per Serving: 183 kcal, 16 g fat, 2 g saturated fat, 12 g carbohydrate, 8 g fibre, 3 g protein.

 Healthy Tip: Avocados are rich in monounsaturated fats that benefit your blood lipid levels. Use this recipe as a vegetable dip, or as a spread for whole-wheat crackers, chips or tortillas to make healthy snacks.

Cumin Crusted Fish

Serves 4 - Serving Size: 4 oz (115 g) fish fillet

Ingredients:

½ -1 Tbsp	ground cumin	7.5-15 mL
¼ tsp	thyme	1 mL
1 tsp	paprika	5 mL
½ tsp	lemon pepper	2 mL
1 lb	white fish fillets (walleye, halibut, cod, etc.)	450 g
1 ½ tsp	canola oil	7 mL
2 Tbsp	chopped parsley lemon or lime wedges	30 mL

Directions:

1. In a small bowl, mix together cumin, thyme, paprika, and lemon pepper.

2. Rub spice mixture on both sides of fish fillets.

3. In a large skillet, set over medium heat, heat canola oil. Add fish fillets and cook until browned on both sides and fish is opaque in the centre, about 4 minutes per side.

4. Sprinkle with parsley and serve immediately with lemon or lime wedges.

 About This Recipe: Herbs are the main influence of this easy-to-make meal. White fish is high in protein and is light on flavour making it ideal for the various flavours of cumin, thyme, paprika, parsley and lemon!

Per Serving: 180 kcal, 9 g fat, 1 g saturated fat, 0.9 g carbohydrate, 0.7 g fibre, 23 g protein.

 Quick Tip: Instead of potatoes and broccoli, try asparagus, carrots and other vegetables as a side dish. Also, you can replace the dinner roll with half of a whole-wheat pita.

Week 4, Day 5

Meal	Ingredients per Serving	Canada's Food Guide Servings
Breakfast Mushroom Omelette (recipe follows)	1 serving Mushroom Omelette 1 slice pumpernickel bread 1 tsp (5 mL) non-hydrogenated margarine ½ cup (125 mL) orange juice 1 cup (250 mL) coffee / tea 2 Tbsp (30 mL) 1% milk (optional) 1 tsp (5 mL) granulated sugar (optional)	2 ½ Vegetables and Fruit 1 Grain Products 1 Meat and Alternatives 1 Oils and Fats
Morning Snack Yogurt and Cereal	1 oz (30 g) All-Bran Buds ¾ cup (175 mL) low-fat yogurt	1 Grain Products 1 Milk and Alternatives
Lunch Turkey Sandwich and Crunchy Vegetables	2 slices whole-wheat bread 2 slices 1.5 oz (40 g) low-fat cheese of choice 2.5 oz (70 g) sliced cooked turkey 1 Tbsp (15 mL) low-fat mayonnaise 1 Tbsp (15 mL) cranberry sauce 1 cup (250 mL) mixed raw vegetables such as snow peas, baby carrots, turnip sticks, cauliflower or broccoli florets, bell peppers 1 Tbsp (15 mL) ranch dressing	2 Vegetables and Fruit 2 Grain Products 1 Meat and Alternatives 1 Milk and Alternatives 1 ½ Oils and Fats
Afternoon Snack Graham Crackers with Cantaloupe and Milk	½ cup (125 mL) fresh cantaloupe 4 graham crackers ½ cup (125 mL) 1% milk	1 Vegetables and Fruit 1 Grain Products ½ Milk and Alternatives
Dinner Savory Beef and Beans in Wine Sauce with Three Pepper Coleslaw (recipes follow)	1 serving Savory Beef and Beans in Wine Sauce 1 serving Three Pepper Coleslaw 1 whole-wheat dinner roll	2 Vegetables and Fruit 2 Grain Products ½ Meat and Alternatives 1 Oils and Fats
Evening Snack Pecan Pumpkin Bran Muffin with Blueberries and Tea (recipe follows)	1 Pecan Pumpkin Bran Muffin ¼ cup (60 mL) blueberries ½ cup (125 mL) 1% milk	1 Vegetables and Fruit 1 Grain Product ½ Milk and Alternatives
Total Servings:		8 Vegetables and Fruit 8 ½ Grain Products 2 ½ Meat and Alternatives 3 Milk and Alternatives 3 ½ Oils and Fats

Good To Know

Nutrition facts of the day	Adjusting today's menu
Calories: 1800 Fat: 43 g Saturated fat: 12 g Carbohydrate: 264 g Fibre: 36 g Protein: 99 g	*To cut about 200 calories* · Cut the serving size of mushroom omelette in half (saves 70 kcal) · Reduce cheese to ¾ oz (22 g) (1 slice) at lunch (saves 35 kcal) · Have only 2 crackers at afternoon snack (saves 60 kcal) · Have half a dinner roll (saves 40 kcal) *To add about 200 calories* · Add ⅓ cup (75 mL) fresh cantaloupe to morning snack (adds 15 kcal) · Add 1 Tbsp (15 mL) peanut butter to afternoon snack (adds 90 kcal) · Drink a cup (250 mL) of 1% milk at dinner (adds 100 kcal)

Mushroom Omelette

Serves 1 - Serving Size: 1 omelette

Ingredients:

2	**eggs**	2
1 Tbsp	**1% milk**	15 mL
¼ cup	**mushrooms, sliced**	60 mL
½ cup	**fresh spinach, roughly chopped**	125 mL

Directions:

1. Whisk eggs and milk together.

2. Pour mixture into skillet on medium heat. Cook until eggs set.

3. Spread mushrooms and spinach on half. Fold omelette in half and leave on heat until eggs are fully cooked.

About This Recipe: Start your day off right with a serving of veggies paired with protein from eggs, to break the night's fast.

Per Serving: 158 kcal, 10 g fat, 3 g saturated fat, 3 g carbohydrate, 0.8 g fibre, 14 g protein.

Healthy Tip: Did you know mushrooms are the only vegetable that contains vitamin D? Mushrooms are also a rich source of B vitamins. Add vitamin A from the spinach and this omelette is vitamin-rich.

Savory Beef and Beans in Wine Sauce

Serves 6 - Serving Size: 1 ½ cups (375 mL) sauce with noodles

Ingredients:

1	egg white	1
¼	package onion soup mix	¼
¼ cup	quick-cooking oats	60 mL
½ lb	extra lean ground beef or ground turkey	225 g
	canola oil cooking spray	
1	medium carrot	1
3	baby potatoe, optional	3
¼ cup	onion, chopped	¼
1	clove garlic, minced	1
½ cup	Great Northern beans or mixed beans, rinsed and drained	125 mL
½ tsp	dried marjoram	2 mL
¼ tsp	dried thyme	1 mL
½ tsp	ground pepper	2 mL
¼ cup	low-sodium beef broth	60 mL
½ cup	red wine or low-sodium beef broth	125 mL
¼ cup	ketchup	60 mL
3 cups	cooked egg noodles	750 mL

Directions:

1. In a small bowl combine the egg whites, onion soup mix and oats. Crumble ground beef (or turkey) over mixture and mix well. Shape into eight 1-inch (2.5 cm) balls.

2. Lightly spray a large non-stick skillet with canola oil cooking spray. Cook beef (or turkey) balls uncovered for 10-15 minutes, browning evenly on all sides.

3. Remove meatballs from pan. Lightly sauté carrots, potatoes if using, onions and garlic.

4. Return meatballs to pan. Add beans, spices, beef broth, red wine and ketchup and simmer until broth mixture is reduced.

5. Serve mixture over hot cooked egg noodles

 About This Recipe: This meatball dish is sure to be a family favourite. Oats and veggies are a great source of fibre and complete this balanced meal.
Per Serving: 270 kcal, 3 g fat, 0.4 g saturated fat, 41 g carbohydrate, 5 g fibre, 18 g protein.

 Healthy Tip: Add extra carrots to increase the vitamin A content of this recipe!

Three-Pepper Coleslaw

Serves 8 - Serving Size: Approximately 1 cup (250 mL)

Ingredients:

1	10 oz (280 g) package angel hair coleslaw mix	1
1	medium red pepper, finely chopped	1
1	medium green pepper, finely chopped	1
1-2	jalapeno peppers, seeds and ribs removed, finely chopped	1-2
3	green onions, chopped	3

Dressing:

¼ cup	white wine vinegar	60 mL
2 Tbsp	lime juice	30 mL
2 tsp	canola oil	10 mL
1 tsp	granulated sugar	5 mL
½ tsp	salt	2 mL
¼ tsp	pepper	1 mL

Directions:

1. Place the first five ingredients - coleslaw mix, peppers and onions in a large serving bowl.

2. In a small bowl whisk the dressing ingredients together. Pour over the coleslaw mixture; toss to coat.

3. Cover and refrigerate for at least 30 minutes before serving.

 About This Recipe: This coleslaw also pairs great with Fish Tacos (see week 2 recipes) for a Mexican-inspired dish.
Per Serving: 151 kcal, 1 g fat, 0.1 g saturated fat, 28 g carbohydrate, 0.8 g fibre, 0.6 g protein.

 Quick Tip: Feel free to substitute any type of coleslaw or broccoli mix for angel hair coleslaw in this recipe. Sweet and chili peppers make this recipe very high in vitamin C.

Pecan Pumpkin Bran Muffins

Serves 18 - Serving Size: 1 muffin

Ingredients:

	canola oil cooking spray	
1 cup	bran cereal	250 mL
1 ¼ cups	non-fat buttermilk	300 mL
1 cup	all-purpose flour	250 mL
⅓ cup	granulated sugar	75 mL
1 Tbsp	baking powder	15 mL
½ tsp	baking soda	2 mL
¼ tsp	salt	1 mL
2 tsp	ground cinnamon	10 mL
2 Tbsp	canola oil	30 mL
2	large egg whites	2
1 Tbsp	vanilla	15 mL
1 cup	pumpkin puree (not pumpkin pie mix)	250 mL

Topping:

¼ cup	pecan pieces	60 mL
2 Tbsp	granulated sugar	30 mL
½ tsp	ground cinnamon	2 mL

Directions:

1. Preheat oven to 400°F (200°C). Lightly coat muffin tin with canola oil cooking spray and set aside.

2. In small bowl, combine bran and buttermilk, stir until moistened and let stand for 5 minutes.

3. Meanwhile, in medium bowl, combine the flour, sugar, baking powder, baking soda, salt and cinnamon; stir until well blended.

4. Add canola oil, egg whites, vanilla and pumpkin to bran mixture. Stir until well blended. Add the pumpkin mixture to the flour mixture and stir until just blended. Do not overmix.

5. Spoon batter into muffin tin. Sprinkle pecan pieces evenly over all. In small bowl, combine the second amounts of sugar and cinnamon. Sprinkle evenly over all and bake for 15 minutes or until wooden toothpick inserted comes out almost clean. Let stand in muffin tins on cooling rack for 15 minutes before carefully removing and cooling completely on rack. To maximize freshness, store muffins covered in refrigerator or freeze.

About This Recipe: You'll never think of bran muffins as boring again! Pecan and pumpkins make these an excellent choice for a nutritious evening snack.

Per Serving: 100 kcal, 3 g fat, 0.3 g saturated fat, 17 g carbohydrate, 3 g dietary fibre, 2 g protein.

Cook Once, Eat Twice or More: One of these muffins, along with ¾ cup (175 mL) of yogurt and ½ cup (125 mL) fruit, add up to a breakfast later in the week.

About Fats and Trans Fats

Fats are energy dense nutrients that are a part of a healthy diet. The terms "saturated fats" and "unsaturated fats" are commonly used when describing the types of fats in food; the less well understood fats are the "trans fats."

Foods high in saturated fats are solid at room temperature, like a block of butter or the fat you can see on a steak. Foods high in unsaturated fats are usually liquid at room temperature like olive oil, canola oil and soybean oil.

Trans fats have some structural characteristics of unsaturated fats but they have become altered, either industrially or naturally, to be more solid at room temperature. This gives these fats highly sought after baking qualities of being solid and shelf stable at room temperature combined with that "melt in your mouth" quality.

Industrial trans fats were developed to convert an over-abundant supply of unsaturated fats into fats with these valuable baking qualities. Trans fat food sources include breaded fried foods, commercially baked goods, hard margarines and other processed foods. However, research has shows that consumption of industrial trans fats may lead to increased risk of chronic illnesses such as cardiovascular disease, insulin resistance, unhealthy weight gain and immune problems. This has led Health Canada to recommend limiting intake to <2 g per day.

Naturally occurring trans fats are formed in the digestive tract of certain animals (e.g. cattle and sheep). Examples of foods that contain some naturally occurring trans fats include: milks, cheeses yogurts, beef and lamb. These trans fats are incorporated into the meat, milk and milk products of these animals. Researchers at the University of Alberta and elsewhere have found that the small quantities of these natural trans fats in foods may have anti-cancer properties and provide some protection from cardiovascular disease.

Avoid consuming industrial trans fats by reading nutrition labels for trans fat content and avoid packaged or processed food containing 'partially hydrogenated' oils or fats. Look for products containing 'non-hydrogenated' oils or fats. Other ways to avoid industrial trans fats are to prepare meals at home with whole foods and, when grocery shopping, avoid the aisles where the processed foods are displayed and concentrate on the outer aisles where the fresh and unprocessed foods are displayed.

Week 4, Day 6

Meal	Ingredients per Serving	Canada's Food Guide Servings
Breakfast Three Cheese Tomato Melt (recipe follows)	1 serving Three Cheese Tomato Melt ½ cup (125 mL) 1% milk 1 cup (250 mL) coffee / tea 2 Tbsp (30 mL) 1% milk (optional) 1 tsp (5 mL) granulated sugar (optional)	¼ Vegetables and Fruit 2 Grain Products 1 ½ Milk and Alternatives 1 Oils and Fats
Morning Snack Vegetable Pita	½ cup (125 mL) carrot sticks ½ cup (125 mL) broccoli or celery 1 Tbsp (15 mL) low-fat ranch dressing ½ whole-wheat pita	2 Vegetables and Fruit 1 Grain Products 1 Oils and Fats
Lunch Spinach Salad with Grilled and Fresh Fruit (recipe follows)	1 serving Spinach Salad with Grilled and Fresh Fruit 2 Tbsp (30 mL) roasted almonds 2 slices pumpernickel bread 2 tsp (10 mL) non-hydrogenated margarine 1 cup (250 mL) 1% milk	2 Vegetables and Fruits 2 Grain Products ½ Meat and Alternatives 1 Milk and Alternatives 3 Oils and Fats
Afternoon Snack Lentil Muffin with Yogurt (see week 2)	1 Lentil Muffin ¾ cup (175 mL) low-fat yogurt	1 Grain Products 1 Milk and Alternatives
Dinner Broiled Trout with Lemon Oil and Oven-Grilled Vegetables (recipe follows)	1 serving Broiled Trout with Lemon Oil and Oven-Grilled Vegetables ½ cup (125 mL) wild rice	3 Vegetables and Fruit 1 Grain Products 2 ½ Meat and Alternative 2 Oils and Fats
Evening Snack Power Smoothie (recipe follows)	1 serving Power Smoothie	¾ Vegetables and Fruit ¼ Milk and Alternatives
Total Servings:		8 Vegetables and Fruit 7 Grain Products 3 Meat and Alternatives 3 ¾ Milk and Alternatives 7 Oils and Fats

Good To Know

Nutrition facts of the day	Adjusting today's menu
Calories: 2261 Fat: 113 g Saturated fat: 15 g Carbohydrate: 231 g Fibre: 21 g Protein: 91 g	*To cut about 200 calories* · Have only 1 slice pumpernickel bread at lunch (saves 65 kcal) · Reduce yogurt to ½ cup (125 mL) at afternoon snack (saves 35 kcal) · Reduce trout to 4 oz (120 g) per serving at dinner (saves 95 kcal) *To add about 200 calories* · Add a mandarin orange to breakfast (adds 45 kcal) · Add ¾ oz (22 g) low-fat shredded cheddar cheese to the pita at morning snack (adds 40 kcal) · Have ¼ cup (60 mL) hummus with lunch (adds 100 kcal)

Three Cheese Tomato Melt

Serves 2 - Serving Size: 1 bagel or English muffin with topping

Ingredients:

¼ cup	shredded cheddar cheese	60 mL
2 Tbsp	shredded part-skim mozzarella cheese	30 mL
1 Tbsp	grated Parmesan cheese	15 mL
2 Tbsp	low-fat mayonnaise	30 mL
⅛ tsp	garlic powder	0.5 mL
4 slices	tomato	4 slices
2	whole grain / wheat bagels or English muffins, split and toasted	2

Directions:

1. Combine cheeses, mayonnaise and garlic powder; set aside.

2. Place a tomato slice on each bagel half; broil 5 inches from the heat for 1-2 minutes or until tomato is warm.

3. Spread about 1 Tbsp (15 mL) cheese mixture over each tomato; broil for 2-3 minutes longer or until cheese is melted.

About This Recipe: What's not to love about this cheesy version of the classic toasted tomato sandwich?

Per Serving: 240 kcal (with English muffin), 8 g fat, 2 g saturated fat, 32 g carbohydrate, 5 g fibre, 13 g protein.

Healthy Tip: Try using at least one low-fat option for one of the cheeses and replace the Parmesan with chopped green veggies to make this breakfast more heart-healthy.

Spinach Salad
with Grilled and Fresh Fruit

Serves 4 - Serving Size: Approximately 1 ½ cups (375 mL)

Ingredients:

	canola oil cooking spray	
¼ cup	raspberry blush vinegar	15 mL
1 Tbsp	granulated sugar	15 mL
1 Tbsp	canola oil	5-10 mL
1-2 tsp	grated fresh gingerroot	
2 slices	fresh pineapple, about ½-inch (1 cm) thick, or two medium peaches, pitted and halved	2 slices
4 cups	loosely packed spinach	1 L
¼ cup	thinly sliced onion	60 mL
1 cup	quartered strawberries	250 mL

Directions:

1. Coat grill or grill pan with canola oil cooking spray and preheat to medium-high.

2. Combine vinegar, sugar, canola oil, and ginger in a small jar, secure lid tightly, and shake vigorously until completely blended. Place pineapple slices or peach halves on plate; brush 1 Tbsp (15 mL) vinegar mixture evenly over both sides.

3. Place pineapple or peaches on grill rack and grill for 4 minutes or until soft and slightly browned. Turn and cook for an additional 4 minutes or until heated through. Cut fruit into bite-size pieces.

4. Place spinach and onion on a serving platter. Top with grilled fruit, sprinkle strawberries evenly on top, and drizzle remaining dressing over all.

 About This Recipe: The vitamin C in strawberries and pineapple helps us absorb the iron in spinach! This salad is ideal for summer barbecues, but can be enjoyed any time of the year.

Per Serving: 124 kcal, 4 g fat, 0.3 g saturated fat, 23 g carbohydrate, 3 g fibre, 1 g protein.

 Quick Tip: Be creative on the grill. Try nectarines, pears, or even orange slices. Brushing the fruits with a small amount of canola will prevent them from sticking to the grill.

 Chef's Tip: No raspberry blush vinegar? Use regular raspberry, or white balsamic vinegar, or rice vinegar instead.

Broiled Trout with
Lemon Oil and Oven-Grilled Vegetables

Serves 4 - Serving Size: 6 oz (170 g) trout

Ingredients:

Canola Lemon Oil:

1 cup	canola oil	250 mL
2 Tbsp	zest of two lemons	30 mL

Trout and Grilled Vegetables:

2	small zucchini, cut in half length-wise, then cut into ¼-inch (0.5 cm) thick diagonal pieces	2
1 pint	grape tomatoes	500 mL
1	medium red onion, cut in half and thinly sliced into half moons	1
4	garlic cloves, peeled and smashed	4
2 sprigs	fresh rosemary	2 sprigs
1 Tbsp	balsamic vinegar	15 mL
2 Tbsp	lemon canola oil	30 mL
½ tsp	salt	2 mL
½ tsp	freshly ground black pepper	2 mL
4	6 oz (170 g) each rainbow trout, whole or fillets	4
2 tsp	lemon oil (see step 1)	10 mL
4 sprigs	fresh rosemary, 2-inches (5 cm)	4 sprigs
½ tsp	freshly ground black pepper	2 mL
	lemon wedges for garnishing	

Directions:

1. To make lemon oil, combine canola oil and lemon zest in a blender. Process until smooth, then strain through fine mesh strainer. Store in refrigerator in airtight container or covered jar for 1-2 days.

2. Preheat broiler. In large bowl, combine zucchini, grape tomatoes, red onion, garlic and rosemary. Drizzle vegetable mixture with balsamic vinegar and lemon canola oil. Toss, then sprinkle with salt and pepper.

3. Spread vegetables in single layer on baking sheet and place 4-inches (10 cm) under broiler for 10 minutes or until vegetables are tender crisp and browned. Halfway through cooking time, toss vegetables.

4. While vegetables are cooking, prepare baking sheet with foil and canola oil. Place trout fillets on prepared baking sheet. Sprinkle both sides with pepper and place rosemary sprig under each fillet. Drizzle each fillet with ½ tsp (2 mL) lemon canola oil. Place trout under broiler for 7-8 minutes or until fish is opaque and flaky.

5. Carefully lift trout from baking pan with spatula and serve with vegetables.

About This Recipe: Rainbow trout is a member of the salmon family and is an excellent source of omega-3 fatty acids, which help to prevent heart disease and have many other health benefits.

Per Serving: 365 kcal, 20 g fat, 4 g saturated fat, 8 g carbohydrate, 2 g fibre, 37 g protein.

Power Smoothie
Serves 2 - Serving Size: 1 cup (250 mL)

Ingredients:

¼ cup	cooked white beans	60 mL
¾ cup	frozen mixed berry concentrate (½ of 341 mL can)	175 mL
½ cup	skim milk	125 mL
1 Tbsp	granulated sugar (optional)	15 mL
½ tsp	vanilla extract	2 mL
5-6	ice cubes	5-6

Directions:

1. Place white beans and juice in blender. Blend well.

2. Add skim milk and vanilla extract. Blend until thick and creamy.

3. Add ice cubes and blend thoroughly.

4. Serve immediately or store in refrigerator. Blend again just before serving.

 About This Recipe: This mighty smoothie lives up to its name. The white beans offer an abundant source of dietary fibre... and you won't even be able to taste the difference!

Per Serving: 236 kcal, 0.8 g fat, 0.1 g saturated fat, 57 g carbohydrate, 2 g fibre, 4 g protein.

 Healthy Tip: Make sure to drink enough water in the day when eating foods high in fibre to avoid constipation.

 Chef's Tip: Smoothies made from beans are a good source of fibre and protein. If you are using dry beans, soak them in water for 12 hours or overnight in the refrigerator - 3 cups (750 mL) of water for every 1 cup (250 mL) of beans. Drain the beans and replace the water before cooking. In a heavy saucepan, combine soaked beans with water and bring to a boil. Cover tightly, reduce heat and simmer until they are just tender and not mushy.

Sources of Week 4 Recipes - From the PANDA Nutrition Team

Lemon Berry Mini Pancakes *(developed by Nancy Hughes)*
Chicken Tikka Masala (*developed by Nancy Hughes)*
Apricot-Ginger Granola *(developed by Nancy Hughes)*
Cumin Corn Chowder *(developed by Nancy Hughes)*
Grilled Sirloin with Fresh Horseradish-Mint Relish *(developed by Nancy Hughes)*
Mushroom Omelette
Back Bacon and Potato Patties *(developed by Nancy Hughes)*
Raspberry Orange Pumpkin Snack Cake *(developed by Nancy Hughes)*
Easy Guacamole
Berry Citrus Brown Betty *(developed by Nancy Hughes)*
Zucchini Bean Casserole *(developed by Nancy Hughes)*

Used with Permission

Alberta Pork Commission: Autumn Pepper Pork Medallions
Canada Beef: Pasta Florentine Bake
Taste of Home Magazine: Three Pepper Coleslaw; Three Cheese Tomato Melt; Garlic Toast
Alberta Pulse Growers: Savoury Beef and Beans in Wine Sauce; Power Smoothie; Zucchini Bean Casserole
CanolaInfo.org: Peppermint Chocolate Chunk Cookies, Breakfast-On-The-Go-Cookies, Cumin Crusted Fish, Spinach Salad with Grilled and Fresh Fruit, Broiled Trout with Lemon Oil and Oven-Grilled Vegetables, Lentil Burritos, Pumpkin Flan, Southwestern Turkey and Bean Salad, Pecan Pumpkin Bran Muffins, Cucumber Snow Peas
Progressive Foods Inc: Mushroom Barley Soup

For more recipes visit: www.pureprairie.ca

Average Intakes of Week 4:

By Food Group:	By Nutrient Profile:
7 Vegetables and Fruit 7 Grains 3 Meat and Alternatives 3 Milk and Alternatives	1899 kcal Total Energy 67 g fat (31% of total energy) 13 g saturated fat (6% of total energy) 243 g carbohydrate (52% of total energy) 37 g fibre 96 g protein (20% of total energy)

Week 4, Day 7

Meal	Ingredients per Serving	Canada's Food Guide Servings
Breakfast Back Bacon and Potato Patties with Milk (recipe follows)	1 serving Back Bacon and Potato Patties ¾ cup (175 mL) 1% milk 1 cup (250 mL) coffee / tea 2 Tbsp (30 mL) 1% milk (optional) 1 tsp (5 mL) granulated sugar (optional)	1 Grain Products ½ Meat and Alternatives ¾ Milk and Alternatives
Morning Snack Cereal and Yogurt	¼ cup All-Bran Buds 2 Tbsp (30 mL) roasted almonds ½ cup (125 mL) low-fat yogurt	½ Grain Products ½ Meat and Alternatives ¾ Milk and Alternatives
Lunch Zucchini Bean Casserole with Toast (recipe follows)	1 serving Zucchini Bean Casserole 1 slice whole-wheat toast ½ cup (125 mL) 1% milk	2 ¾ Vegetables and Fruit 1 ½ Grain Products ¾ Meat and Alternatives ½ Milk and Alternatives
Afternoon Snack Crackers and Cheese	6 whole-wheat crackers (e.g. low-sodium Triscuits) ¾ oz (22 g) low-fat cheddar cheese	1 Grain Products ½ Milk and Alternatives
Dinner Autumn Pepper Pork Medallions and Cucumber with Snow Peas (recipes follow)	1 serving Autumn Pepper Pork Medallions 1 serving Cucumber with Snow Peas ½ cup (125 mL) brown rice or whole-wheat pasta	3 ½ Vegetables and Fruit 1 Grain Products 1 Meat and Alternatives 2 ½ Oils and Fats
Evening Snack Raspberry Orange Pumpkin Snack Cake and Milk (see week 2)	1 serving Raspberry Orange Pumpkin Snack Cake ½ cup (125 mL) 1% milk	½ Vegetables and Fruit ½ Milk and Alternatives
Total Servings:		6 ¼ Vegetables and Fruit 6 Grain Products 2 ¾ Meat and Alternatives 3 Milk and Alternatives 2 ½ Oils and Fats

Good To Know

Nutrition facts of the day

Calories: 1839
Fat: 63 g
Saturated fat: 13 g
Carbohydrate: 240 g
Fibre: 36 g
Protein: 91 g

Adjusting today's menu

To cut about 200 calories
· Skip almonds at morning snack (saves 65 kcal)
· Skip whole-wheat toast at lunch (saves 70 kcal)
· Have 2 rice cakes instead of crackers at afternoon snack (saves 60 kcal)

To add about 200 calories
· Increase milk to 1 cup (250 mL) at lunch (adds 50 kcal)
· Double the amount of pasta in the casserole at lunch (adds 45 kcal)
· Have a medium pear with the afternoon snack (adds 105 kcal)

Back Bacon
and Potato Patties

Serves 4 - Serving Size: 2 patties, 1 oz (28g) back bacon

Ingredients:

1 lb	russet potatoes, shredded	450 g
4 oz	back bacon or extra lean ham, chopped	115 g
½ cup	green onion, chopped	125 mL
1	large egg, beaten	1
¼ tsp	dried thyme	1 mL
⅛ tsp	salt	0.5 mL
¼ tsp	ground black pepper	1 mL
½ tsp	paprika	2 mL
2 Tbsp	canola oil	30 mL

Directions:

1. Preheat oven to 175°F (80°C).

2. Shred potatoes in a food processor or by hand, and pat dry with paper towels. Combine the potatoes with the back bacon, onions, egg, thyme, salt, pepper and paprika in a medium bowl.

3. Heat 1 Tbsp (15 mL) of the canola oil in a large non-stick skillet over medium heat. Spoon half of the potato mixture in 4 mounds in the skillet. Flatten with a fork to make 4-inch (10 cm) patties and cook for 3 minutes on each side, or until golden. Transfer to a heat-proof plate and place in oven to keep warm.

4. Repeat with remaining canola oil and potato mixture.

About This Recipe: These patties are so simple to make! Substitute different spices and herbs for flavour variations each time you cook them.

Per Serving: 206 kcal, 9 g fat, 1 g saturated fat, 22 g carbohydrate, 2 g fibre, 10 g protein.

Quick Tip: Freeze any left-overs for a handy afternoon snack later in the week. Just microwave for approximately 30 seconds to thaw and warm up.

Zucchini Bean Casserole

Serves 4 - Serving Size: Approximately 1 ½ cups (375 mL)

Ingredients:

2 cups	cooked red kidney beans	500 mL
1 tsp	canola oil	5 mL
1	onion, coarsely chopped	1
1	clove garlic, minced	1
6	mushrooms	6
½	medium zucchini	½
1 can	19 oz (540 mL) diced tomatoes	1 can
½ cup	water	125 mL
½ cup	whole-wheat pasta, small shapes	125 mL
1 tsp	ground thyme	5 mL
	salt (optional) and ground black pepper to taste	
½ tsp	ground oregano	2 mL
¼ cup	grated Parmesan cheese	60 mL
2 tsp	dried parsley flakes	10 mL

Directions:

1. Drain and rinse the kidney beans with cold water.

2. In non-stick skillet, heat canola oil over medium heat; cook onion and garlic, stirring occasionally, for about 4 minutes or until onion is translucent.

3. Cut mushrooms into quarters. Cut zucchini lengthwise in half, then into 1-inch (2.5 cm) thick slices. Add mushrooms and zucchini to skillet; cook for 2 minutes.

4. Stir in tomatoes (break them up with a fork), ½ cup (125 mL) water, cooked kidney beans, pasta, thyme, and oregano; season to taste with salt and pepper as desired.

5. Bring to a boil; reduce heat and simmer for 15 minutes or until pasta is al dente (tender but not mushy).

6. Sprinkle each serving with Parmesan cheese and parsley.

 About This Recipe: Parsley and Parmesan add a sharp finishing flavour to this satisfying vegetarian dish.
Per Serving: 266 kcal, 4 g fat, 1 g saturated fat, 43 g carbohydrate, 12 g fibre, 15 g protein.

 Quick Tip: You can also cook the casserole without pasta and serve it over rice or barley. Rice will make this a gluten-free dish, suitable for celiac diets.

Autumn Pepper Pork Medallions

Serves 8 - Serving Size: 3 oz (85 g) pork chop

Ingredients:

1 ½ lbs	pork loin chops or tenderloin, boneless	680 g
½ cup	whole-wheat flour	125 mL
1 cup	sundried tomatoes	250 mL
1 Tbsp	canola oil	15 mL
2 tsp	canola oil	10 mL
24	small mushrooms	24
6	shallots	6
1 ½ cups	low-sodium chicken broth	375 mL
¼ cup	cooking sherry	60 mL
1 tsp	Worcestershire sauce	5 mL
2 Tbsp	fresh parsley, chopped	30 mL
¼ tsp	each dried oregano, basil, thyme, dill rosemary, salt and pepper	1 mL
1 Tbsp	canola oil	15 mL
½	each sweet red, green and yellow pepper	½

Directions:

1. Cut pork into 8 serving size pieces. Flatten pork slices with your hand and toss in flour to coat lightly..

2. Add tomatoes to boiling water for 2 minutes; drain, cool and cut into thin strips.

3. Heat 1 Tbsp (15 mL) canola oil over medium heat and sauté pork for 1 ½ minutes per side; remove from pan and keep warm.

4. Heat 2 tsp (10 mL) oil in pan. Sauté mushrooms for 1-2 minutes. Stir in broth, sherry, tomatoes, Worcestershire sauce, parsley and seasonings. Add pork and simmer for 5-10 minutes.

5. Sauté peppers in 1 Tbsp (15 mL) canola oil and use to garnish pork.

6. Serve over pasta or rice.

 About This Recipe: Enjoy this herb-infused dish of Canadian-raised pork. Adding sautéed vegetables would make this a hearty meal.

Per Serving: 231 kcal, 11 g fat, 2 g saturated fat, 15 g carbohydrate, 3 g protein.

 Chef's Tip: Substitute dry red wine, or broth, for the cooking sherry, if preferred.

Cucumber with Snow Peas

Serves 4 - Serving Size: ½ cup (125 mL)

Ingredients:

2 Tbsp	canola oil	30 mL
1	small onion, finely chopped	1
¼ tsp	crushed red pepper flakes	1 mL
1	medium-sized cucumber, seeded, thickly sliced	1
1 bag	6 oz (170 g) fresh snow peas, snip tips and remove strings	1 bag
1 Tbsp	cider vinegar	15 mL
½ tsp	granulated sugar	2 mL
⅛ tsp	ground ginger	0.5 mL

Directions:

1. In large wok or skillet, heat canola oil.

2. Stir in onion and sauté for 2 minutes. Add crushed pepper and cucumber slices and sauté for 1 minute. Add snow peas and sauté until tender-crisp.

3. Stir in vinegar, sugar and ginger. Serve immediately.

About This Recipe: This crunchy salad makes for an appetizing side dish! Add extra ginger to meet your flavour expectations.

Per Serving: 105 kcal, 7 g fat, 0.5 g saturated fat, 9 g carbohydrates, 2 g fibre, 2 g protein.

Chef's Tip: If you enjoy this side dish, serve it with other meat recipes in the menu plan. Add a serving of grain products and a cup of milk to make it a meal.

Raspberry Orange Pumpkin Snack Cake

Serves 16 - Serving Size: 1 slice with sauce and yogurt

Ingredients:

Cake:

	canola oil cooking spray	
1 pkg	18.25 oz (510 g) spice cake mix	1 pkg
¾ cup	water	175 mL
¼ cup	canola oil	60 mL
4	egg whites or ½ cup (125 mL) egg substitute	4
½ can	15 oz (419 mL) no salt added pumpkin (not pumpkin pie mix)	½ can
2 tsp	grated fresh orange rind	10 mL

Topping:

1 cup	water	250 mL
1 ½ Tbsp	cornstarch	22 mL
2 cups	fresh or frozen unsweetened raspberries (or Saskatoon berries)	500 mL
1 Tbsp	granulated sugar	15 mL
1 cup	non-fat plain greek yogurt, optional	250 mL

Directions:

1. Preheat oven to 325°F (170°C).

2. Coat a 13 x 9 inch (33 x 22 cm) non-stick baking pan with cooking spray.

3. Combine the cake mix, ¾ cup (175 mL) water, oil, egg whites, pumpkin and orange rind in a large bowl. Using an electric mixer, beat according to the package directions. Pour the batter in the pan. Bake for 26-28 minutes or until wooden toothpick inserted in the centre of the cake comes out almost clean. Place on a wire rack and <u>cool completely in pan</u>.

4. Meanwhile, stir together 1 cup (250 mL) water and cornstarch in a medium saucepan until cornstarch is completely dissolved. Add the berries and sugar. Bring to a boil over medium-high heat and boil for 2 minutes or until berries are beginning to soften and break down. Remove from heat. Let cool completely.

5. To serve, top each serving of cake with the berry sauce and yogurt.

About This Recipe: Make an ordinary cake mix into a tasty snack loaded with flavour.

Per Serving: 202 kcal, 7 g fat, 0.8 g saturated fat, 31 g carbohydrate, 2 g fibre, 4 g protein.

APPENDIX
Measurement Tables Equivalents and Conversions

Oven Temperatures

Fahrenheit (°F)	Celsius (°C)
175	80
200	95
225	110
250	120
275	140
300	150
325	160
350	175
375	190
400	205
425	220
450	230
475	240
500	260

Liquid Measurements

Spoons		Cups	
Empirical Measure	Metric Measure	Empirical Measure	Metric Measure
¼ teaspoon (tsp)	1 millilitre (mL)	¼ cup (4 Tbsp, 2 oz)	60 mL
½ tsp	2 mL	⅓ cup	75 mL
1 tsp	5 mL	½ cup	125 mL
1 tablespoon (Tbsp) = 3 tsp	15 mL	1 cup	250 mL

Dry Measures

Empirical Measure	Metric Measure
1 ounce (oz)	28 grams (g)
4 oz	115 g
1 pound (lb, 16 oz)	450 g

Internal Cooking Temperatures

Food	Temperature
Beef, veal and lamb (pieces and whole cuts) – medium-rare	145°F (63°C)
Beef, veal and lamb (pieces and whole cuts) – medium	160°F (71°C)
Beef, veal and lamb (pieces and whole cuts) – well done	170°F (77°C)
Pork (pieces and whole cuts)	160°F (71°C)
Poultry (e.g. chicken, turkey, duck) – pieces	165°F (74°C)
Poultry (whole)	185°F (85°C)
Ground meat and meat mixtures (e.g. burgers, sausages, meatballs, meatloaf, casseroles) – beef, veal, lamb and pork	160°F (71°C)
Ground meat and meat mixtures – poultry	165°F (74°C)
Egg dishes	165°F (74°C)
Others (hot dogs, stuffing and leftovers)	165°F (74°C)

Carbohydrate Counting Information

The Carbohydrate Counting system is an advanced meal planning system for people with diabetes, based on the *"Canadian Diabetes Association, Beyond the Basics: Meal Planning Guide."* It groups foods depending on whether they raise your blood sugar levels or not.

Most of the foods that raise your blood sugar levels are equivalent to 1 carbohydrate choice (15 g of carbohydrate). Fat, protein and fibre do not directly raise or lower blood sugar but they may slow down absorption of sugar in the body. You can use this system to exchange carbohydrate choices, meat & alternatives and fats choices. You will find an example on how to make substitutions using this system and a table with examples of the foods included in each group.

Making substitutions in the menus

Example: If you want to substitute ¼ cup granola in your breakfast for other food:

1. Use Table 1 to identify how many carbohydrate choices are in ¼ cup (60 mL) of granola. In this example, ¼ cup (60 mL) of granola belongs to the group of grains & starches and is equivalent to 1 carbohydrate choice.

2. Exchange for the same number of carbohydrate choices. In this example you could exchange ¼ cup (60 mL) of granola for 1 slice of bread, ¾ cup (175 mL) of oatmeal, etc.

3. You can follow the same procedure to make substitutions for meat & alternatives and for fats.

Meal	Ingredients per Serving	Carbohydrate Counting
Breakfast Breakfast Parfait	½ cup frozen berries ¼ cup low-fat granola ¾ cup low-fat yogurt 1 cup (250 mL) coffee / tea k (optional) d sugar (optional)	3 ½ carbohydrate choice ↓

GRAINS & STARCHES
1 carbohydrate choice =

- 1 slice of bread
- ¾ cup (175 mL) oatmeal (cooked)
- ½ cup corn (kernel)
- ½ cup rice, brown and white (cooked)
- ½ cup wild rice
- ½ cup sweet potato
- ½ medium (84 g) potato
- ½ cup whole-wheat pasta
- ¼ cup granola ←
- 1 small plain muffin

Note: In total this breakfast provides 3 ½ carbohydrate choice.

Table 1: Beyond the Basics
Meal Planning for Healthy Eating, Diabetes Prevention and Management

Use this table to make changes to the menu plan to suit your preferences.

Foods that raise blood sugar levels
(Each serving of these groups contains 15 g of carbohydrates = 1 carbohydrate choice)

Foods that do not directly raise or lower blood sugar

Grains and Starches
1 carbohydrate choice =

- 1 slice of bread
- 3 Tbsp (45 mL) bread crumbs
- ¾ cup (175 mL) oatmeal (cooked)
- ½ cup (125 mL) corn (kernel)
- ⅓ cup (75 mL) rice, brown and white (cooked)
- ½ cup (125 mL) barley (cooked)
- ½ cup (125 mL) wild rice
- ⅓ cup (75 mL) sweet potato
- ½ medium (84 g) potato
- ½ cup (125 mL) whole-wheat pasta
- ¼ cup (60 mL) granola
- 1 small plain muffin
- ½ whole-wheat pita or tortilla
- 2 rice cakes
- 1 small whole grain dinner roll
- ½ whole-wheat English muffin
- ½ cup (125 mL) bran flakes
- 7 multigrain or whole-wheat soda crackers or melba toast
- ½ whole grain bagel
- 1 all bran bar or granola bar
- 1 medium pancake
- 2 small oatmeal raisin cookies
- 3 cups (750 mL) popcorn
- 1 oz (30 g) of cereal

Meat and Alternatives
1 Meat and Alternatives choice =

- ⅓ of a 6.5 oz (180 g) can tuna or salmon
- ⅓ cup (75 mL) feta
- ⅓ cup (75 mL) hummus
- 1 oz (30 g) of pork, chicken, ham, beef turkey, fish
- 1 large egg
- ¼ cup (60 mL) 1% cottage cheese
- 2 Tbsp (30 mL) peanut butter
- 1 oz (30 g) mozzarella, cheddar, monterey jack cheese
- 1 oz (30 g) ground beef
- ⅓ cup (85 g) tofu
- ½ cup (125 mL) lentils, chickpeas, kidney beans, black beans
- 2 Tbsp (30 mL) Parmesan cheese

Fruits (Fresh, frozen or canned)
1 carbohydrate choice =

- 2 cups (500 mL) strawberries, raspberries or cranberries
- 1 cup (250 mL) blueberries, Saskatoon berries
- 1 cup (250 mL) of peach slices or 1 peach
- 1 small apple, pear, orange
- 1 cup (160 g) cantaloupe, cubes or balls
- ½ cup (125 mL) applesauce, unsweetened
- 3 Tbsp (23 g) dried cranberries
- 2 Tbsp (18 g) raisins
- 1 small or ½ large banana
- ½ cup (125 mL) canned fruit salad (in water)
- ½ cup (125 mL) orange or apple juice
- 1 small grapefruit

Fats
1 fats choice =

- 1 tsp (5 mL) margarine
- 8 large black olives
- 1 tsp (5 mL) oils (canola, olive)
- 1 Tbsp (15 mL) low-fat mayonnaise
- 7 pieces (10 g) almonds
- ¼ oz (7 g) pecans, dry roasted, approximately 4 nuts
- ⅓ oz (10 g) walnuts, black, approximately 5 nuts
- ½ oz (15 g) pumpkin seeds, approximately 1 Tbsp
- 2 Tbsp (30 mL) low-fat salad dressing
- 2 Tbsp (30 mL) spreadable cheese (light)
- 1 tsp (5 mL) salad dressing regular
- 2 Tbsp (30 mL) low-fat sour cream
- ⅓ avocado

Table 1: Beyond the Basics (Continued...)
Meal Planning for Healthy Eating, Diabetes Prevention and Management

Use this table to make changes to the menu plan to suit your preferences.

Foods that raise blood sugar levels (Each serving of these groups contains 15 g of carbohydrates = 1 carbohydrate choice)	Foods that do not directly raise or lower blood sugar
Milk and Alternatives 1 carbohydrate choice =	**Vegetables**
¾ cup (175 mL) low-fat yogurt 1 cup (250 mL) 1% or skim milk ½ cup (125 mL) evaporated milk 1 cup (250 mL) soy milk	With the exception of parsnips, peas, turnips and squash which **do** affect blood sugar more than other vegetables when more than ½ cup (125 mL) is consumed.
	1 vegetable choice = 1 cup (250 mL) of: romaine lettuce, cucumber, tomato, green beans, spinach, red bell peppers, sprouts, onion, celery, zucchini, broccoli, carrots, cauliflower, mushroom, brussels sprouts, squash, 4 spears asparagus
Other Choices (To be used occasionally and in moderation) 1 carbohydrate choice =	**Extras** 1 fats choice =
1 Tbsp (15 mL) sugar or brown sugar 1 Tbsp (15 mL) maple syrup / honey 2 Tbsp (30 mL) low sugar jam, jelly or marmalade 1 Tbsp (15 mL) regular jam, jelly or marmalade	Some of these foods, when consumed in large amounts, may affect blood sugar*
	1 Tbsp (15 mL) ketchup*
	coffee
	tea
	vinegar
	cinnamon
	low fat balsamic vinaigrette
	broth

Adapted from the Canadian Diabetes Association *Beyond the Basics*

Index by Meal

How to use this index: Ingredients are arranged by Food Groups, followed by the name of the recipe, the page number on which it is found and the menu (week, day) in which it can be found. In addition, ingredients forming parts of menus but not included in a recipe are listed by the meal and menu (week, day) where they are used. This way, you can see how frequently a particular ingredient is used and whether a substitution might be more practical. The focus of this list is perishable foods. Refer to the Pantry List on page 7 for staple items used in PPEP recipes.

Index by Ingredient - Vegetables and Fruit (Continued...)

Index by Ingredient - Grains

* Whole wheat bread is used very frequently and is not included in the index. For most recipes, you can readily substitute bagels and English muffins, or pitas and tortillas.

** Pasta and Rice are non-perishable and are listed in the Pantry list on Page 7.

Index by Ingredient - Meat and Alternatives

Index by Ingredient - Milk and Alternatives

* Choose low-fat options most often. Unsweetened yogurt and sour cream may be substituted in most cases.
**Parmesan Cheese is listed under Condiments and Oils in the Pantry list on Page 7.